Music for Sight Singing

Third Edition

Thomas Benjamin

The Peabody Conservatory
of the Johns Hopkins University

Michael Horvit

Moores School of Music
The University of Houston

Robert Nelson

Moores School of Music
The University of Houston

D1292046

Wadsworth
Thomson Learning™

Australia • Canada • Mexico • Singapore • Spain • United Kingdom • United States

Music Publisher: Clark Baxter

Senior Development Editor: Sharon Adams Poore

Assistant Editor: Cherie Hackelberg

Editorial Assistant: Jennifer Ellis

Marketing Assistant: Cara Durr

Print Buyer: Stacey Weinberger

Permissions Editor: Joohee Lee

Production Service: Greg Hubit Bookworks

Autography: Mansfield Music-Graphics
  (for music new to third edition)

Cover Designer: The Visual Group

Compositor: TBH Typecast, Inc.

Printer: Transcontinental Printing

For permission to use material from this text, contact us by

  Web: http://www.thomsonrights.com
  Fax: 1-800-730-2215
  Phone: 1-800-730-2214

For more information, contact

Wadsworth/Thomson Learning
10 Davis Drive
Belmont, CA 94002-3098
USA
http://www.wadsworth.com

International Headquarters
Thomson Learning
290 Harbor Drive, 2nd Floor
Stamford, CT 06902-7477
USA

UK/Europe/Middle East/South Africa
Thomson Learning
Berkshire House
168–173 High Holborn
London WC1V 7AA
United Kingdom

Asia
Thomson Learning
60 Albert Street #15-01
Albert Complex
Singapore 189969

Canada
Nelson Thomson Learning
1120 Birchmount Road
Toronto, Ontario M1K 5G4
Canada

Contents

Part I Common Practice Techniques: Diatonic

Part II Common Practice Techniques: Chromatic

Part III Twentieth-Century Techniques

Preface

Music for Sight Singing is intended to be used over a two- or three-year span. Parts I and II parallel the typical common practice two-year theory sequence. Part III may be integrated into the two-year sequence or may be used in a separate course dealing specifically with twentieth-century materials. The order of *Music for Sight Singing* parallels that of our other texts, *Techniques and Materials of Tonal Music* and *Music for Analysis,* but the text can easily be used with most other theory textbooks.

As with our earlier texts, *Music for Sight Singing* grew out of our collective teaching experience at the Moores School of Music, The Peabody Conservatory of Music, and the institutions with which we were previously connected. A particular advantage of *Music for Sight Singing* is that the authors are all practicing composers.

The book consists primarily of newly written exercises and melodies that are graded and cumulative and that isolate the particular musical devices under study. Every effort has been made to compose material that is musically and stylistically appropriate as well as pedagogically suitable.

In *Music for Sight Singing,* we have included both part music from the literature and newly composed material. As in our *Music for Analysis,* the music from the literature has been carefully selected to be appropriate and workable at the student's level of progress. We feel that it is important to expose the student to a wide variety of vocal part music from the standard repertoire. All other material has been originally composed to control its content. We have been very careful to compose original material that, in addition to being carefully graded and cumulative, is musical and stylistically diverse.

As the student works through the text, each aspect of music reading is isolated and presented in a specific set of exercises. Problems of rhythm, meter, and pitch are dealt with separately and then together. The melodies and part music are appropriately edited with tempo designations, dynamics, and articulations to encourage the student to deal with all aspects of musical notation while sight singing.

We wish to thank the following people for their help in the preparation of the first edition: Edward Haymes and Luisa Chomel for help with translations; and George S. T. Chu, Hamline University; John C. Nelson, Georgia State University; Dorothy Payne, Department of Music, The University of Texas at Austin; Emily Romney, Longy School of Music, Cambridge, Mass.; and Scott Wilkinson, The University of New Mexico, for their reviews of the manuscript. The reviewers for the second edition were Richard DeVore, Kent State University; Scott Lindroth, Duke University; Rafael Lopez, Community College of Denver; Justus Matthews, CSU Long Beach; and Robert Zierolf, University of Cincinnati. For this third edition, the reviewers were Joel Galand, University of Rochester; Phillip Schroeder, Sam Houston State University; and Robert Zierolf, University of Cincinnati.

Thomas Benjamin　Michael Horvit　Robert Nelson

Suggestions to the Teacher and Student

To the Teacher

The following are some suggestions for the optimum use of this book. We have used three types of exercises:

1. *Unpitched rhythmic exercises,* which provide practice with specific rhythmic problems. Included among these are canons and duets. The duets may be performed with individuals or groups on each part. Or each student may perform both parts, either by vocalizing one part and tapping the other, or by tapping both parts, one with each hand.
2. *Pitched preliminary exercises,* which isolate specific melodic and harmonic problems. These should be mastered before going on to the melodies.
3. *Melodies (canons, duets, and trios),* specifically composed to deal in a musical way with material presented in the preliminary exercises.

Interspersed throughout the exercises are units containing vocal part music from the literature. These provide a more complete musical context for the materials studied thus far.

1. It is important that some material from each section of each unit be covered, and in the proper order. More exercises are contained in each section than most classes will have time to use. It is not necessary to complete all the preliminary exercises before going on to the melodies in each unit. The intent here is to provide teachers with the flexibility to meet their individual needs.
2. We strongly recommend that students *conduct* all exercises and melodies after the concept of meter is introduced. The teacher should present preparatory beats, fermatas, and cutoffs. A useful procedure is to have various students conduct the class in the part music. Preliminary exercises are intended both as a presentation of specific materials and for drill on those materials, as distinct from the melodies and part music. With all material, a balance between sight reading in class and outside preparation is desirable.
3. In singing pitched material, it is possible to use a variety of methods: fixed or movable *do,* numbers, or a neutral syllable, such as *la.* Tonally oriented systems, such as movable *do* and numbers, work very well in primarily diatonic contexts; however, they lose their efficacy in highly modulatory materials and most twentieth-century idioms.
4. The tessitura of some exercises and melodies may be difficult for some students. These may be sung in any comfortable register or even transposed to a different key at the teacher's discretion. Instrumental as well as vocal idioms have been used to provide students with experience in dealing with the kinds of materials they are likely to encounter in performance situations. In the melodies and part music, emphasis should be placed on both accuracy and musicality of performance, including phrasing, articulation, and dynamics.
5. We have employed the normal range of conventional approaches to notation:
   a. Where an incomplete measure occurs at the beginning of an exercise, it is frequently, but not always, balanced metrically in the last measure.
   b. Cautionary accidentals have been indicated both with and without parentheses.
   c. Clef changes within a given melody will occur both within and between phrases.
   d. The variety of notational conventions in twentieth-century music is illustrated in Part III.

6. This book may be used with a wide variety of theory texts currently available. In large measure, it is structured to parallel the organization of the authors' *Techniques and Materials of Tonal Music,* fifth edition (Wadsworth, 1998), and may be used to reinforce the concepts presented therein.

7. Students should be urged to analyze the music they sing in class, including basic melodic shape and structural pitches, harmonic implications, phrase and period structure, cadences, motives, counterpoint, and style.

Because the development of aural skills–the ability to hear and recognize intervals or common chord progressions, to transcribe melodies, and even to hear and transcribe simple pieces–is such an important complementary skill to sight singing, we strongly recommend the systematic use of ear-training drills to accompany the singing exercises in this book. And though *Music for Sight Singing* is designed specifically as a sight-singing text, the exercises can be adapted for use in melodic or rhythmic dictation, using those materials that are not sung in class. The exercises can also be adopted for keyboard harmony by using the melodies for harmonization in a variety of textures and styles.

We recommend that the following Suggestions to the Student be discussed in class as early as possible in the course.

To the Student

The ability to read accurately and fluently at sight is essential to your musicianship; the competent musician must be able to translate symbol into sound with speed and precision. The exercises in this book have been written and selected to provide you with a wide variety of typical musical problems and to provide exposure to many different styles, materials, and techniques.

You should practice sight reading daily, just as you would practice your own instrument or voice. Steady, disciplined work will yield the best and longest-lasting results. Practice all examples only as fast as you can perform them with accuracy.

Here are some suggestions for practicing and performing the music in this book.

1. *Rhythmic reading.* The rhythmic exercises may be performed in several different ways, for example:

    clapping or tapping the rhythm

    tapping the rhythm while conducting

    vocalizing (as on *ta*) the rhythm while conducting

    tapping the beat with one hand and the rhythm with the other

    tapping or clapping the rhythm while counting aloud the beats in each measure

The rhythmic duets may be performed with one person performing both parts, using a combination of tapping and vocalizing, or with a different person on each part. In general, be as metronomic and rhythmically precise as possible; you may profitably use a metronome while practicing.

Common conducting patterns are shown on page viii. Compound duple meters, such as $\frac{6}{8}$ or $\frac{6}{4}$, are conducted in either 2 or 6, depending on tempo. Compound triple meters may be conducted in either 3 or a subdivided 3, and compound quadruple in either 4 or a subdivided 4. In slow tempos, simple meters may be conducted with a divided beat.

Quintuple meters, such as $\frac{5}{4}$, may be conducted as shown in the illustration, or as combinations of duple and triple meters. Similarly, septuple meters, such as $\frac{7}{4}$, may be conducted as a combination of duple, triple, and/or quadruple.

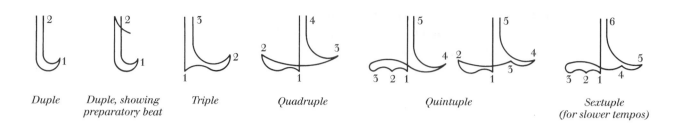

Duple   Duple, showing   Triple   Quadruple   Quintuple   Sextuple
         preparatory beat   (for slower tempos)

2. *Reading of melodies and part music.* This is one possible technique for sight singing:
   a. Note the meter signature and decide on an appropriate conducting pattern. Look up any unfamiliar tempo designations in the glossary.
   b. Find, analyze, and drill any rhythmic problems.
   c. Determine the key and play the tonic pitch on a piano or other instrument. Sing the tonic triad, and find the first note of the melody.
   d. Sing and conduct through the exercise at a moderate tempo, concentrating on accuracy of pitch and rhythm. Mark breathing places.
   e. Isolate and drill any pitch problems. Use the piano or instrument very sparingly, if at all, and only to check your pitch. The less you use it, the better.
   f. Conduct and sing through the exercise again as musically as possible, observing all dynamic, tempo, phrasing, and articulation markings.

In each sight-singing exercise:
   a. Concentrate on accurate intonation.
   b. Work for steady tempo and rhythmic accuracy.
   c. For musicality, observe all performance markings and the musical style of each example; work for continuity and a clear sense of phrase.
   d. Keep your eyes moving ahead of where you are singing. As your sight reading improves, train your eyes to scan ahead over the next several notes and ultimately over several measures. The farther you are "ahead of yourself," the better your sight reading will be. Train yourself to recognize melodic patterns, such as scale fragments, chord arpeggiations, repetitions, sequences, cadential formulas, and so on. It is both easier and more musical to perform patterns than to merely move from note to note.
   e. Try "silent singing," in which you conduct through an exercise and sing it internally; then check it by singing aloud. This is a very good exercise for improving your "internal ear."
   f. Remember: "Find it, don't fake it." If you are not sure of the next pitch, find it by relating it to a previous pitch either by interval or by relation to the tonic note.

3. *Analysis.* It is a very good idea to analyze the melodies and part music you are performing. Such analyses not only will make it easier to read well but also will increase your awareness of style, musical materials, and techniques. The following points should be noted:
   a. Phrase structure, including cadence placement and types, and periodic structures, if any.
   b. Patterns, such as repetitions, sequences, and returning pitches, which both unify the melody and make it easier to read.
   c. Motivic content.
   d. Structural pitches, the principal notes that give a melody its overall shape and direction.

e. Harmony. As appropriate, analyze the underlying harmonies implied by the melodic lines, being attentive to the patterns of nonharmonic tones. This will improve your understanding of the relation of harmony to melody, will increase your ability to harmonize melodies quickly and musically, and will make it easier to sing.

Here is a sample analysis of a melody, with structural pitches circled:

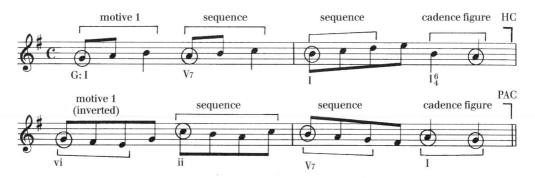

4. This book does not depend on any particular singing system. At the discretion of the teacher, you may use scale-degree numbers, note names, a neutral syllable such as *la,* or the *fixed do* or *movable do* system of *solfège* syllables. We suggest that you initially approach an unfamiliar clef by singing the exercises using note names.

The syllables for the *movable do* system are

The syllables indicated for the chromatic scale as shown here on *C* are those used in the *fixed do* system.

Alternative syllables for minor scales are

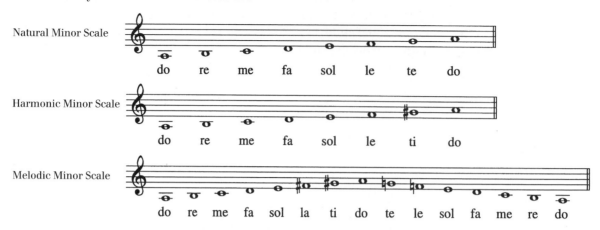

Natural Minor Scale

do re me fa sol le te do

Harmonic Minor Scale

do re me fa sol le ti do

Melodic Minor Scale

do re me fa sol la ti do te le sol fa me re do

In the *fixed do* system, the syllables always coincide with the letter names of the notes, regardless of key. For example, *C* is always do and *F* is always fa, and so on.

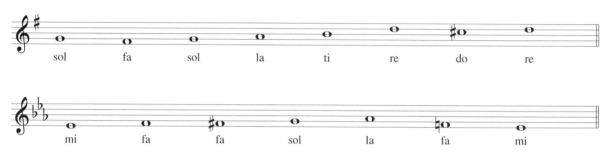

sol fa sol la ti re do re

mi fa fa sol la fa mi

It is also possible to use the *fixed do* system with inflected syllables, as given in the chromatic scale above.

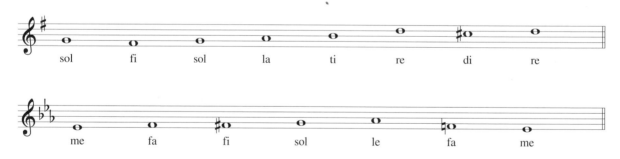

sol fi sol la ti re di re

me fa fi sol le fa me

Part I

Common Practice Techniques:
Diatonic

1

Rhythm: One- and Two-Pulse Units (Unmetered)

Preliminary Exercises

These exercises introduce one- and two-pulse rhythmic values. They may be performed in a variety of ways, for example, by tapping or clapping the pulse while vocalizing the rhythm.

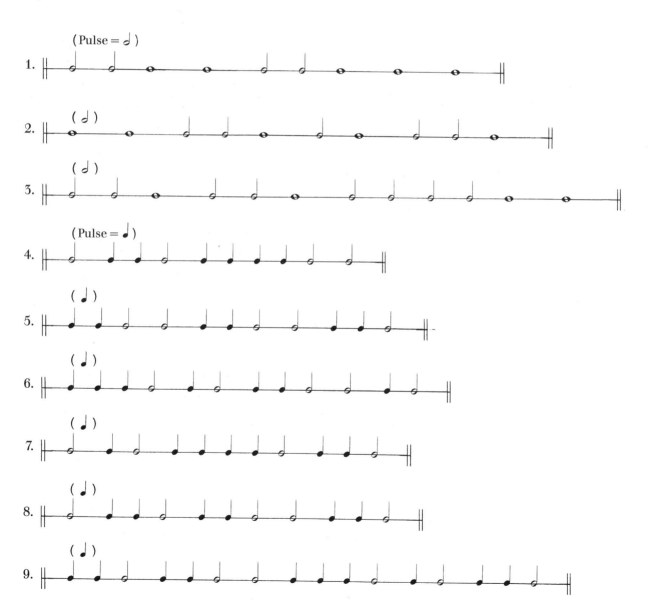

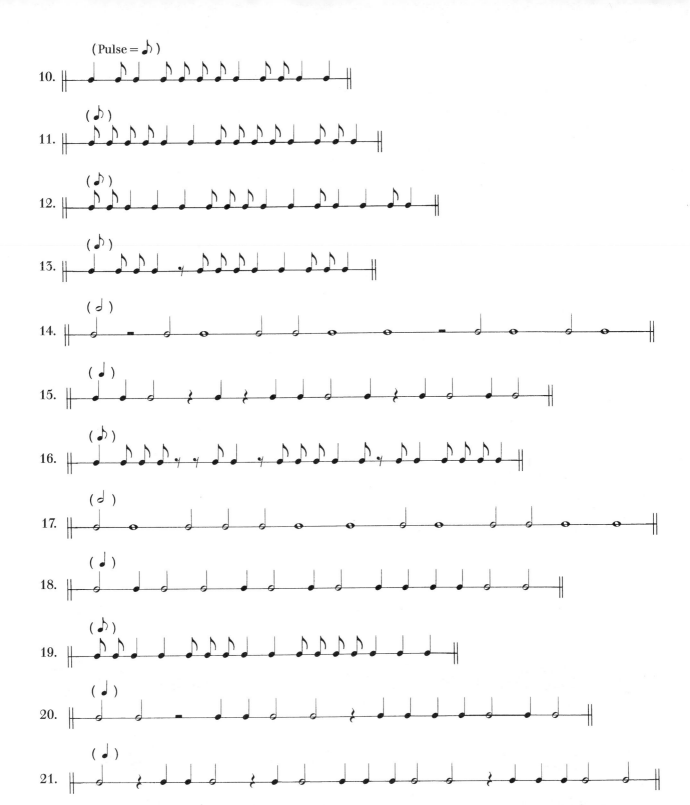

Rhythmic Duets

Rhythmic duets may be performed in the following ways:

1. Separate people vocalizing, tapping, or clapping each part.

2. Each student performing both parts, using some combination of tapping, clapping, or vocalizing.

Pitch: The Major Scale

Preliminary Exercises

These exercises contain only *conjunct* (stepwise) motion. They should be performed by tapping or clapping the pulse while singing the pitches, using scale-degree numbers, a neutral syllable, fixed *do,* or movable *do.*

4

Melodic Exercises

For ways of preparing the melodic exercises, see Suggestions to the Student, pp.vii–x.

Duets

2

Rhythm: Simple Meters

Preliminary Exercises

These exercises introduce simple meters. They should be performed by conducting the meter while vocalizing the rhythm. For conducting patterns, see Suggestions to the Student, pp. vii–x.

10. 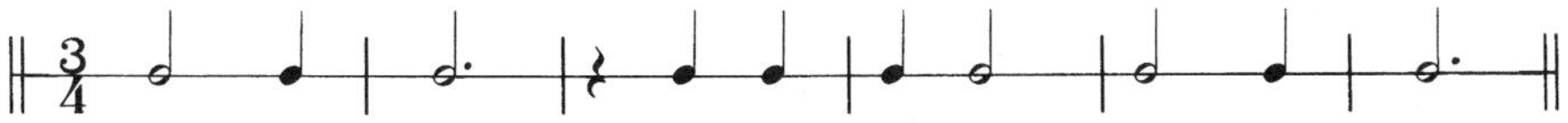

11. 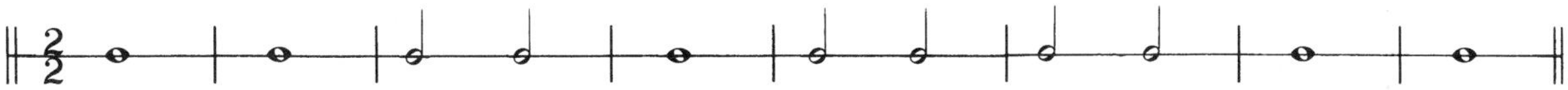

12. 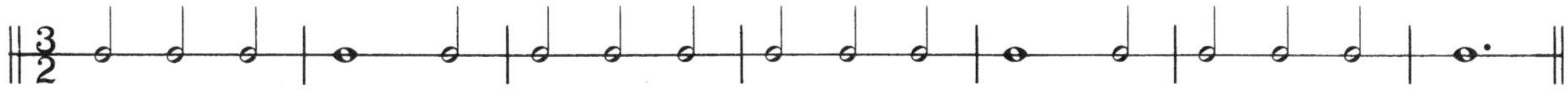

13. 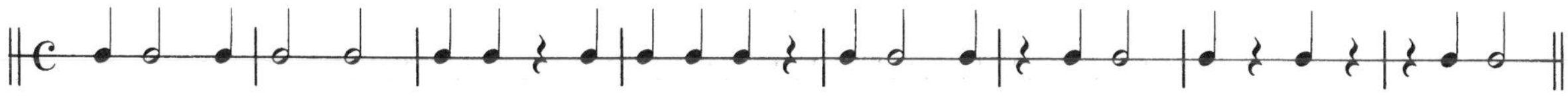

14. 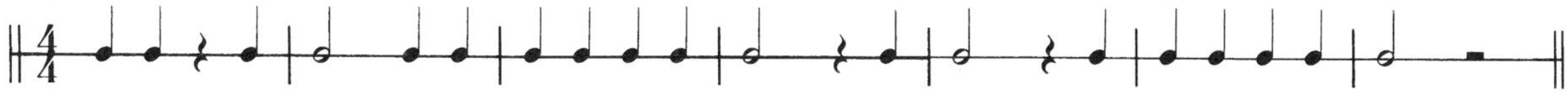

15. 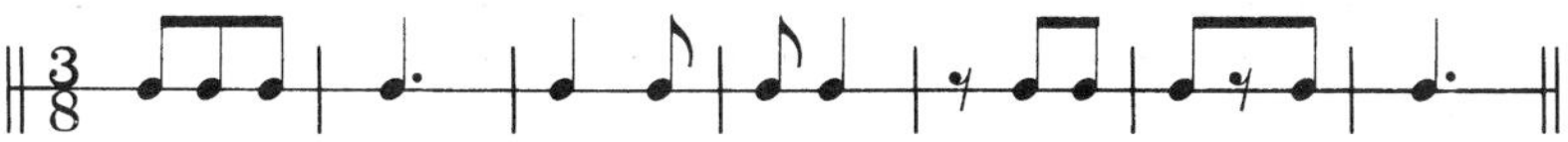

16. 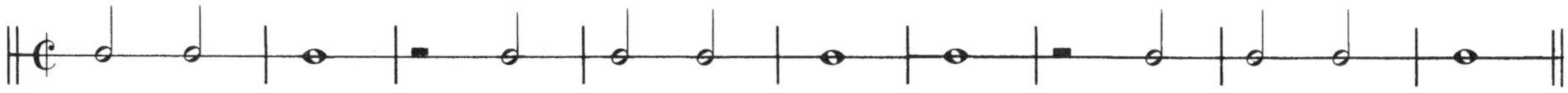

17. 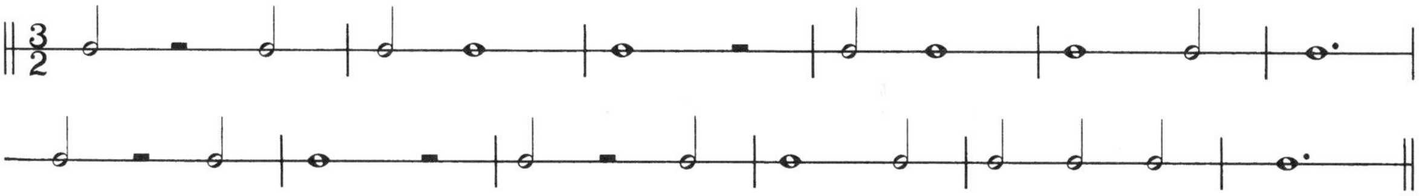

Canon

18. 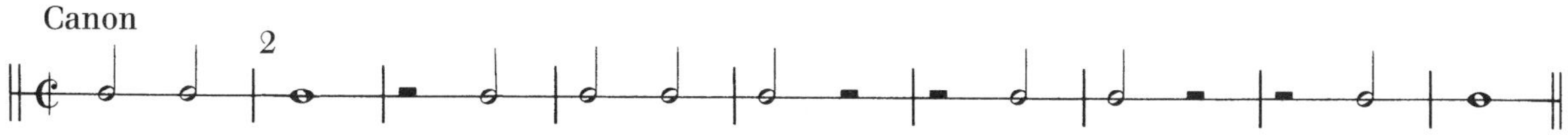

Canon

19. 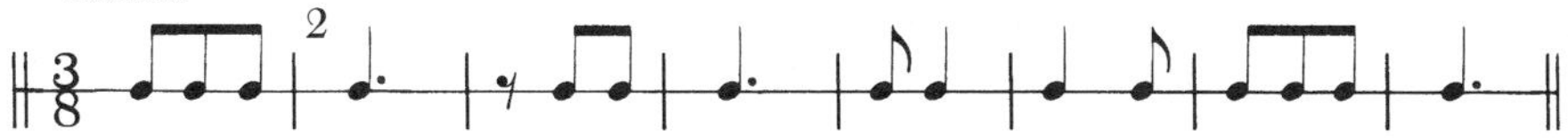

Canon

20. 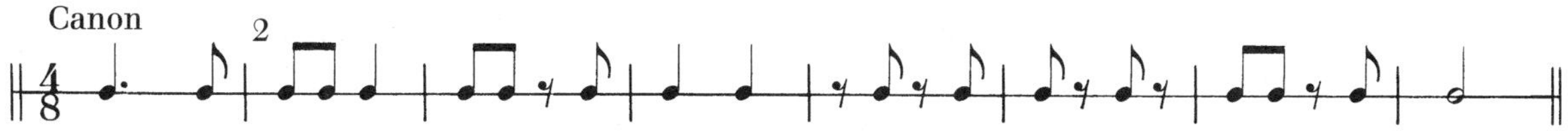

Canon

21. 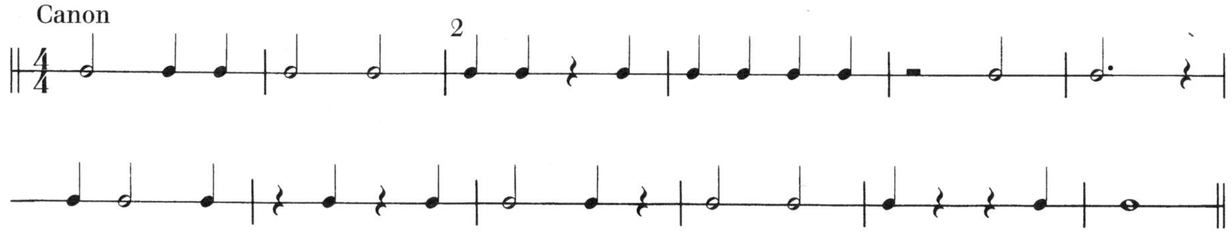

Rhythmic Duets

These duets may be performed in the usual ways: separate people vocalizing, tapping, or clapping each part; or each student performing both parts, using some combination of clapping, tapping, or vocalizing.

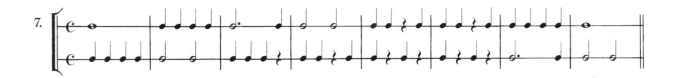

Pitch: Introducing Thirds

Preliminary Exercises

All metered melodies should be conducted as they are being sung.

Pitch: Introducing Fourths

Preliminary Exercises

Melodies

These and all subsequent melodies should be performed in as musical a manner as possible, with attention to phrasing, dynamics, and tempo markings. Careful analysis of the melodies will be helpful. For procedures for preparation and analysis, see Suggestions to the Student, pp. vii–x.

17

Semplice

12.

Ben marcato

13.

Klingend

14.

Adagio sostenuto

15.

Vif

16.

Andantino

17.

Duets

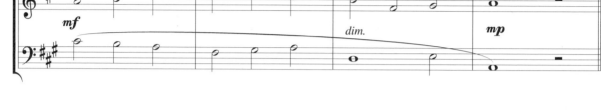

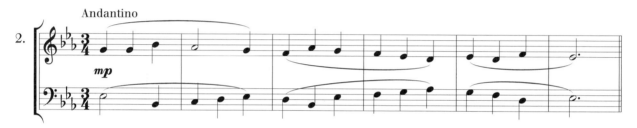

3

Pitch: Tonic Triad in the Major Mode; Introducing Fifths, Sixths, and Octaves

Preliminary Exercises

Melodies

24

25

Canons and Duets

4

Rhythm: 2:1 Subdivisions of the Beat

Preliminary Exercises

In addition to the usual method of performing these exercises (conducting and vocalizing),
it may be useful to tap the subdivisions of the beat.

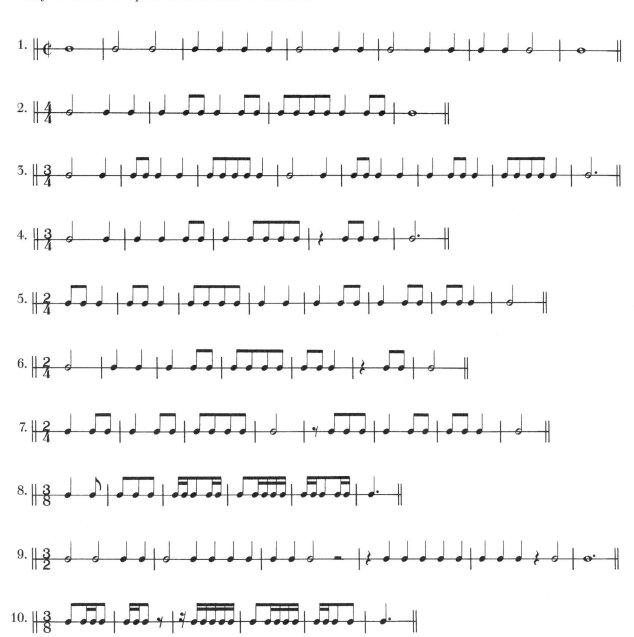

11. 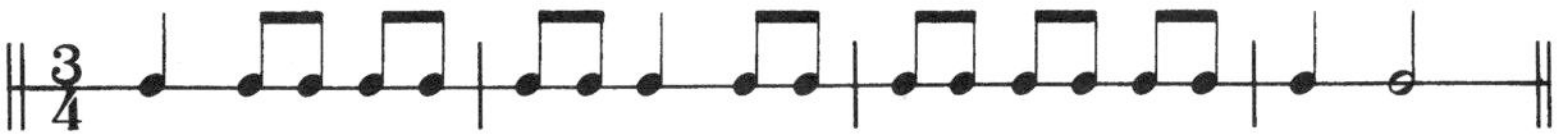

12. 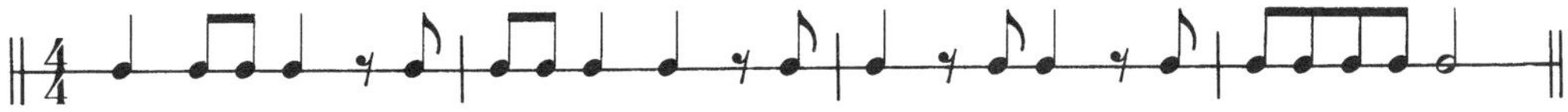

13. 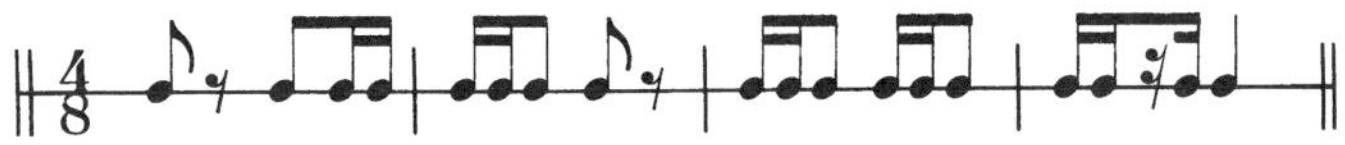

14. 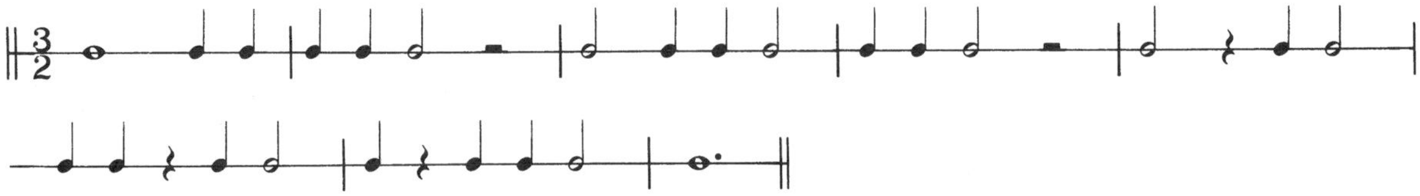

15. 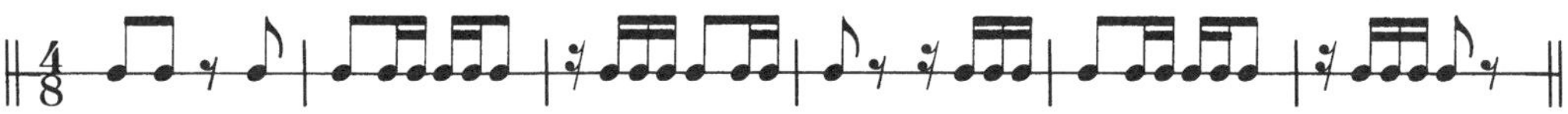

16. 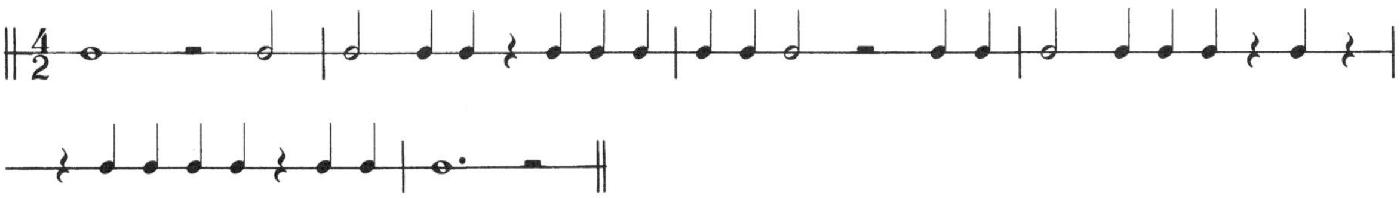

17. 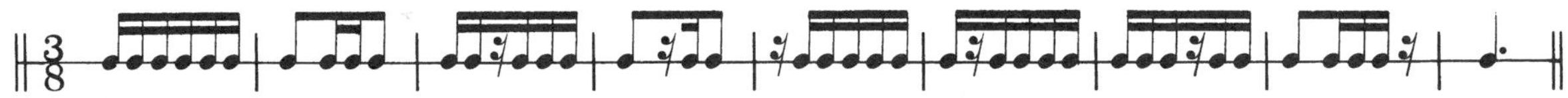

18. 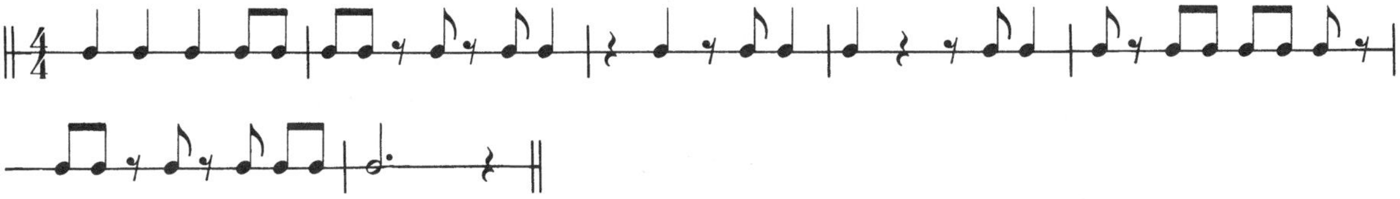

19. 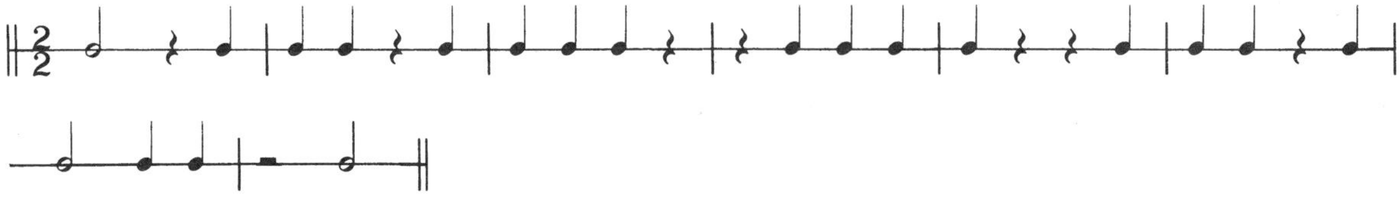

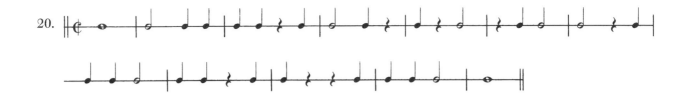

21.

22.

Canon

23.

Canon

Rhythmic Duets

Canon

1.

Pitch: I, V, and V_7; Introducing Sevenths

Preliminary Exercises

Careful consideration of the harmonic implications is useful in singing these exercises. Note that the V_7 will not always appear in its complete form melodically. It is possible to analyze the upper three tones of the V_7 as a vii°.

7.

8.

9.

10.

11.

12.

13.

14.

15.

Melodies

34

35

Duets and Canons

Part Music

5

Rhythm: Anacruses (Upbeats)
and 4:1 Subdivisions of the Beat

Preliminary Exercises

40

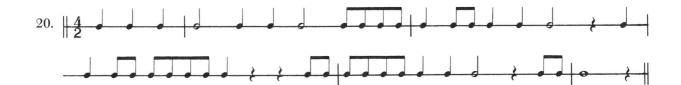

Canons and Duets

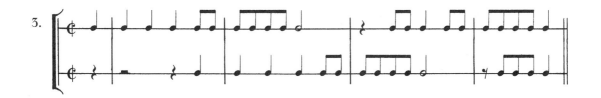

42

Pitch: I, IV, V, and V₇

Preliminary Exercises

9.

10.

11.

12.

13.

14.

15.

44

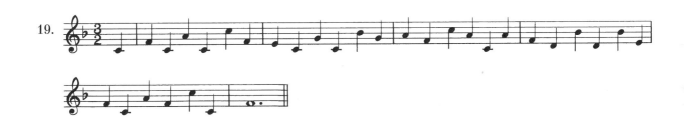

Pitch: Introducing the Alto Clef

Preliminary Exercises

When learning a new clef, it is helpful at first to sing the exercises using the letter names of the notes. Be sure not to think of the new clef as a transposition of a more familiar clef.

4.

5.

6.

7.

8.

9.

10.

11.

12.

13.

14.

Melodies

49

Canons and Duets

Walzer

6.

Allegretto

7.

8.

Bewegt

Part Music

Chorale

1.

6

Rhythm: Dots and Ties

Preliminary Exercises

9. 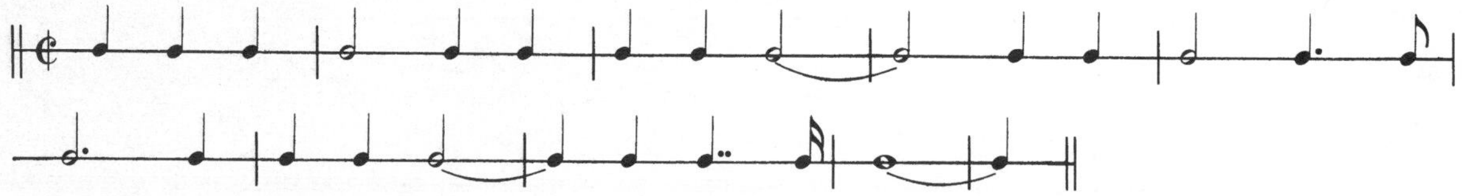

10. 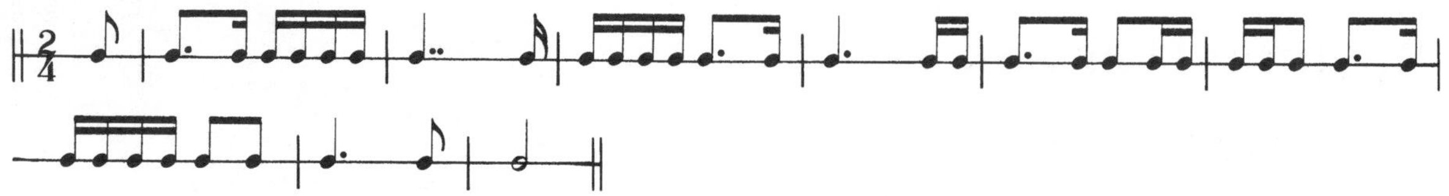

11. 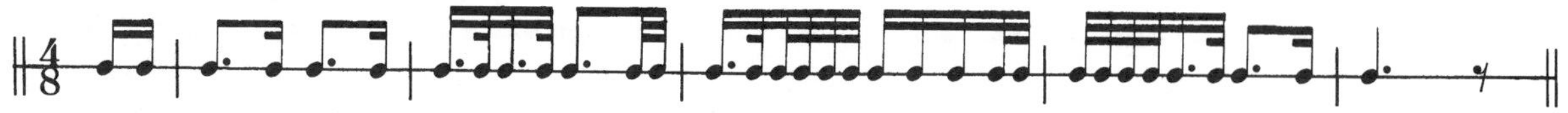

12. 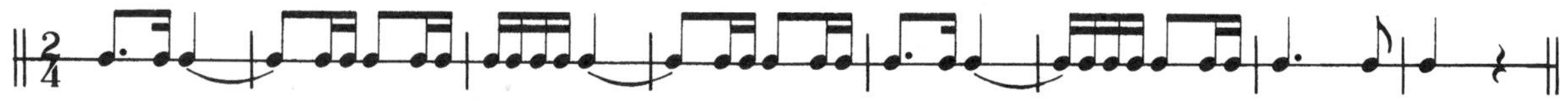

13. 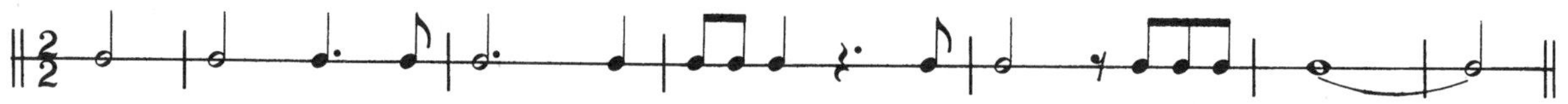

14. 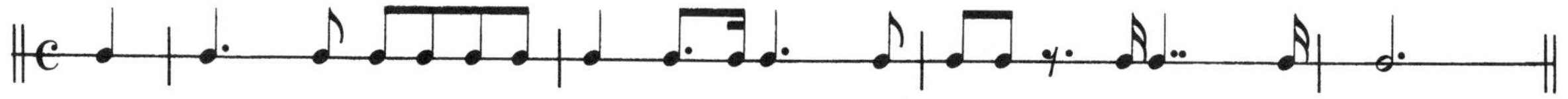

15. 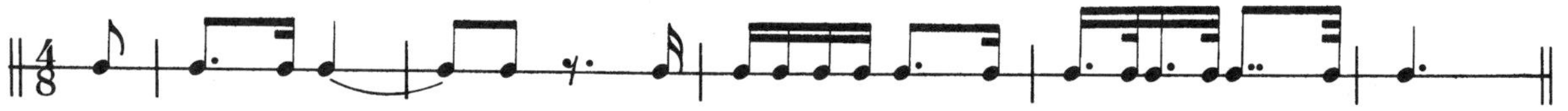

16. 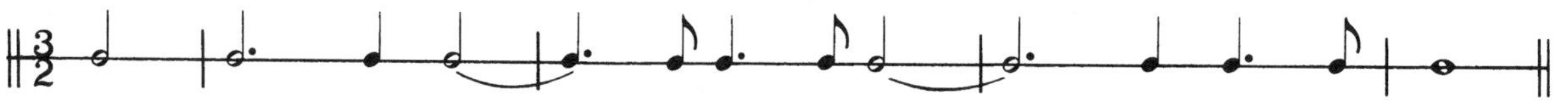

17. 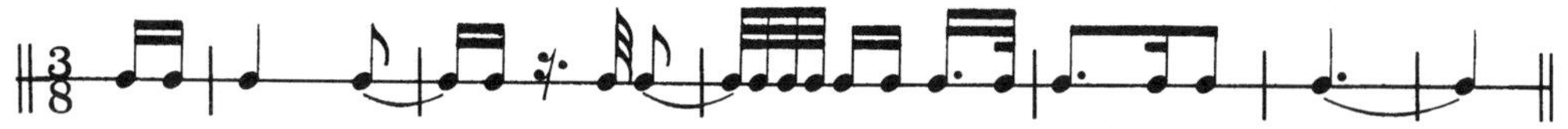

18. 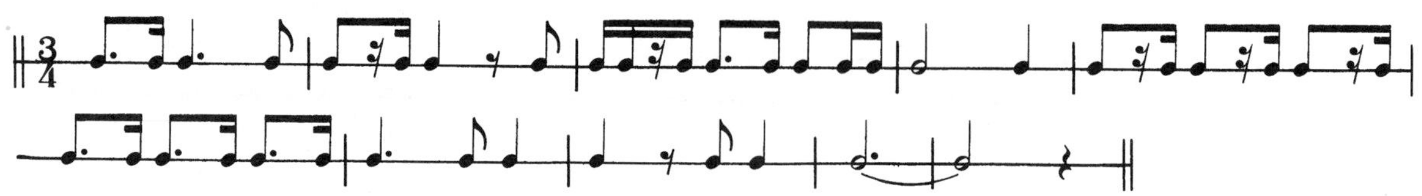

Canons and Duets

Pitch: Minor Mode

Preliminary Exercises

For the *solfège* syllables for inflected scale degrees in the minor mode, see p. x.

12.

13.

14.

15.

16.

17.

18.

19.

20.

Melodies

1.

Duets and Canons

66

Rasch

Etwas fröhlich

Part Music

7

Music from the Literature

4. David Melvill, *To Portsmouth*

To Ports - mouth! To Ports - mouth! it is a gal - lant town: And there we will have a quart of wine with a nut - meg brown. Did - dle down! The gal - lant Ship, the Mer - maid, the Li - on, hang - ing stout. Did make us to spend there our six - teen pence all out.

5. Haydn, *The Lovely Month of May*

The love - ly month of May in - vites to dance and play. Come, join our mer - ry dance, let us skip and let us prance, and woe to those who look a - skance!

6. Mozart, *Difficile lectu*

Dif - fi - ci - le le - ctu mi - hi mars et jo - ni - cu jo - ni - cu dif - fi - ci - le, le - ctu le - ctu le - ctu mi - hi mars, mi - hi mars le - ctu le - ctu dif - fi - ci - le. Le - ctu le - ctu

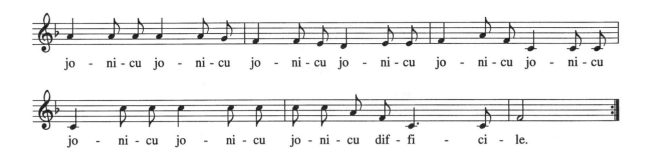

jo - ni - cu jo - ni - cu jo - ni - cu jo - ni - cu jo - ni - cu jo - ni - cu

jo - ni - cu jo - ni - cu jo - ni - cu dif - fi - ci - le.

This is a humorous nonsense Latin text.

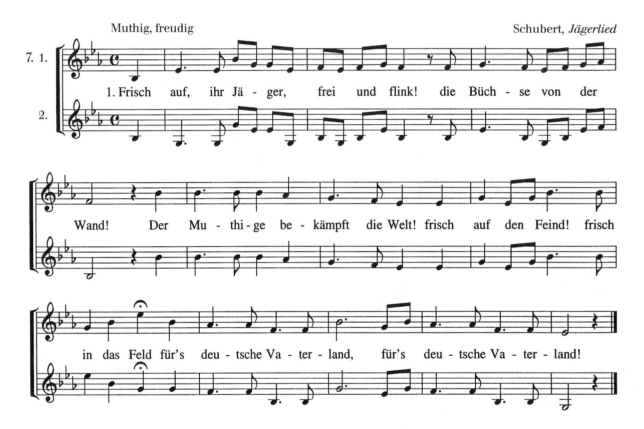

Muthig, freudig

Schubert, *Jägerlied*

7. 1.

1. Frisch auf, ihr Jä - ger, frei und flink! die Büch - se von der

2.

Wand! Der Mu - thi - ge be - kämpft die Welt! frisch auf den Feind! frisch

in das Feld für's deu - tsche Va - ter - land, für's deu - tsche Va - ter - land!

Be quick, you hunters, free and nimble, take the rifle from the wall. The brave conquer the world. Charge the enemy in the field for the German fatherland!

Henry Harrington, *How Great Is the Pleasure*

George A. Minor, *Bringing in the Sheaves*

73

We shall come re - joic - ing, bring - ing in the sheaves. Bring - ing in the sheaves,

bring - ing in the sheaves, We shall come re - joic - ing, bring - ing in the sheaves.

Willy, Prithee Go to Bed

10.

Hey tro lo ly lo ly ly lo ly ly lo ly ly lo ly ly lo ly

Hey ho tro lo ly, tro lo ly ly lo ly ly lo ly

Wil - ly, pri - thee go to bed, For thou wilt have a drow - sy
It is like to be fair weath - er, Coup - le up all thy hounds to -

Hey_____ ho trol - ly, Hey_____ Hey

Schubert, *Willkommen, lieber schöner Mai*

11.

Will - kom - men, lie - ber schön - er Mai, dir tönt der Vö - gel Lob - ge - sang. Will-

Will-

kom - men, lie - ber schö - ner Mai, dir tönt der Vö - gel Lob - ge - sang. Will-

kom - men, lie - ber schö - ner Mai, dir tönt der Vö - gel Lob - ge - sang. Will-

kom - men, lie - ber schö - ner Mai, dir tönt der Vö - gel Lob - ge - sang. Will-

kom - men, lie - ber schö - ner Mai, dir tönt der Vö - gel Lob - ge -. sang. Will-

kom - men, lie - ber schö - ner Mai, dir tönt der Vö - gel Lob - ge - sang. Will-

kom - men, lie - ber schö - ner Mai, dir tönt der Vö - gel Lob - ge - sang. Will-

kom - men, lie - ber schö - ner Mai, dir tönt der Vö - gel Lob - ge - sang. Will-

Welcome, dear, pretty May; to you the birds sing songs of praise.

8

Rhythm: Compound Meter

Preliminary Exercises

These exercises introduce compound meters. The compound duple examples may be conducted in either two or six; compound triple, in three or subdivided three; compound quadruple, in four or subdivided four. Here also it may be useful to tap the subdivisions.

9. 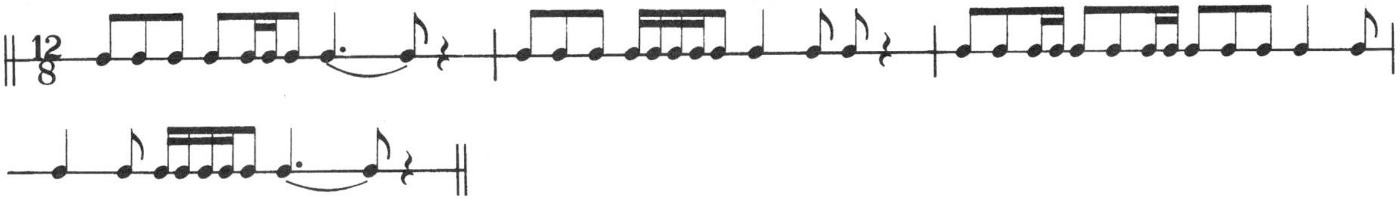

10. 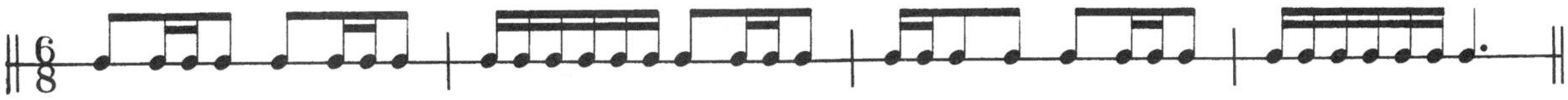

11. 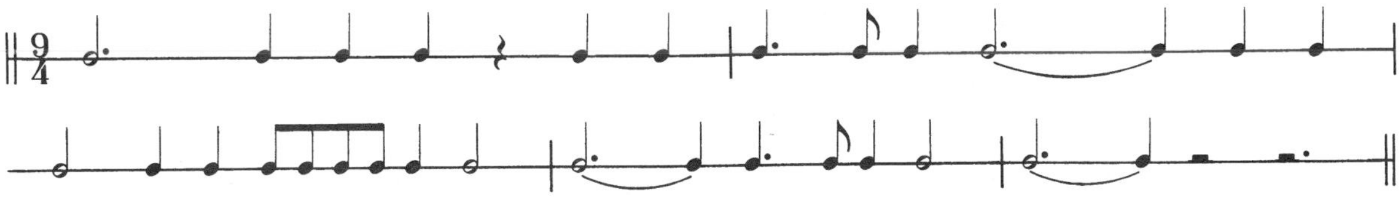

12. 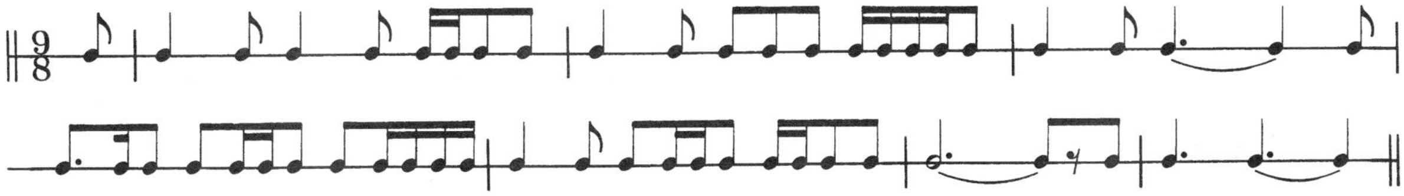

13. 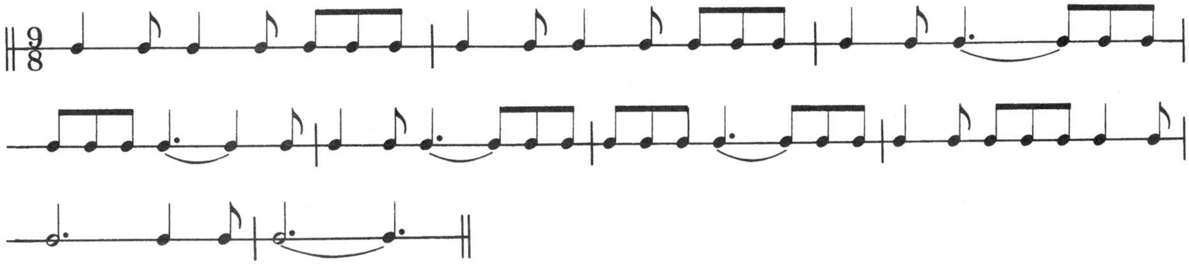

14. 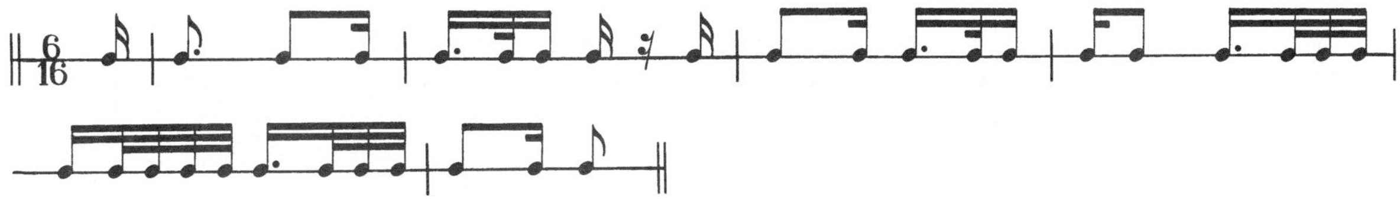

15. 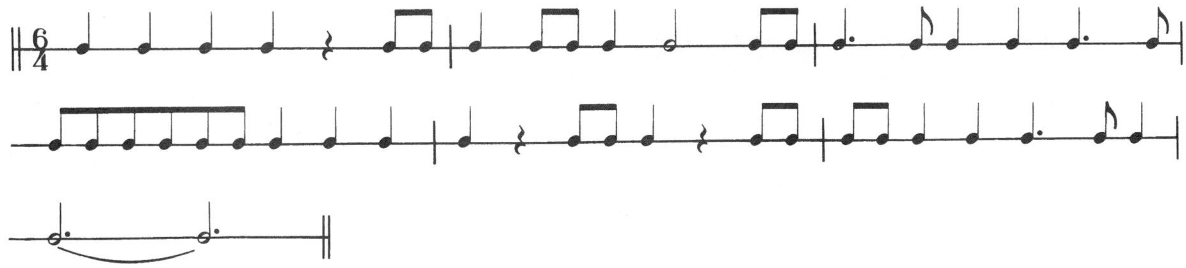

80

Duets

Pitch: Supertonic Triad

Preliminary Exercises

Pitch: Submediant and Mediant Triads

Preliminary Exercises

9.

10.

11.

12.

13.

Pitch: Tenor Clef

Preliminary Exercises

As with the alto clef, it is helpful at first to sing the exercises using the letter names of the notes.

4.

5.

6.

7.

8.

9.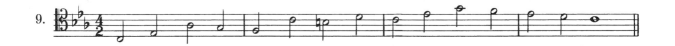

10.

11.

Melodies

1.

89

90

Canons and Duets

Part Music

94

9

Rhythm: Triplets and Duplets

Preliminary Exercises

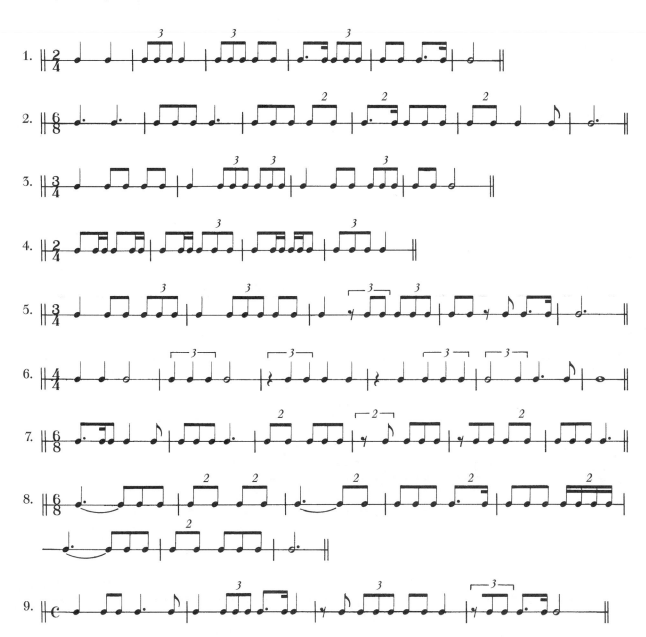

18.

19.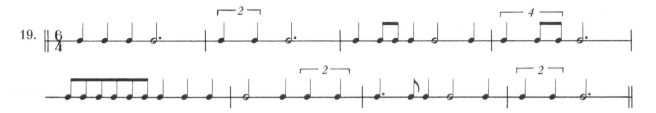

Canons and Duets

1.

2.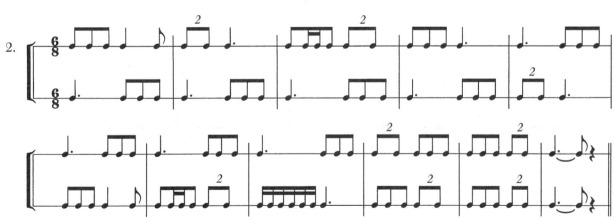

Pitch: Seventh Chords

Preliminary Exercises

Melodies

Smoothly

10

Music from the Literature

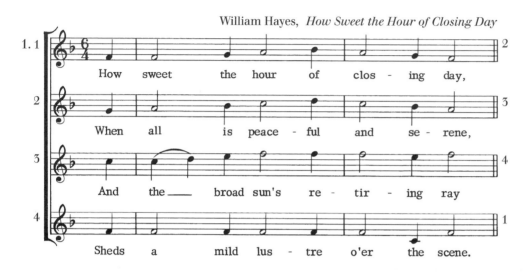

William Hayes, *How Sweet the Hour of Closing Day*

1.1 How sweet the hour of clos - ing day,

2 When all is peace - ful and se - rene,

3 And the broad sun's re - tir - ing ray

4 Sheds a mild lus - tre o'er the scene.

Purcell, *God Save Our Sovereign Charles*

2.1 God save our sov' - reign Charles, our faith's de -

2 Pro - tect Queen Cath' - rine, Eng - land's nurs - ing

3 Who to his pi - ous votes de - nies his

fen - der. Let all good men his laws and ho - nour ten - der.

mo - ther. Pre - serve York's Duke, our King's il - lust - rious bro - ther.

hand. I pray for him too, but wish him out o'th' land.

Melchior Vulpius, *Lo How a Rose*

3.
Lo, how a rose e'er bloom-
A - mid the cold of win-

ing From ten - der root hath
ter When half spent was the

sprung! Of Jes - se's line - age com -
night! A - mid the cold of win -

ing As men of old have sung.
ter When half spent was the night.

John Hilton, *Come, Follow Me!*

4.
1. Come, fol - low, fol - low, fol - low,
2. We have oft been rogues to - geth - er,

Whith - er shall I fol - low, fol - low, fol - low,
We have oft-times nipp'd a bung, boy, Neat - ly,

To the gal - low, gal - low, gal - low,
Neat - ly, neat - ly, neat - ly, neat - ly,

fol - low, fol - low, fol - low me!
Now we must hang 'twixt wind and weath - er:

Whith - er shall I fol - low, fol - low thee?
neat - ly, in a throng, boy, Neat - ly, neat - ly,

To the gal - low, gal - low - tree.
neat - ly, neat - ly, in a throng, boy.

Andantino

Schubert, *Be Welcome*

5.

Singen wir aus Herzensgrund

6.

Was Gott tut, das ist wohlgetan

7.

Freudig

Schubert, *Mailied*

8.

1. Grü - ner wird die Au, und der Him - mel blau! Schwal - ben keh - ren

wie - der und die Erst - ling's lie - der klei - ner Vö - ge -

(Waldhörner)

lein zwit - schern durch_____ den Hain.

The pasture grows greener, and the heavens blue; swallows return, and the songs of the early arrivals twitter through the glade.

Purcell, *At the Close of the Evening*

9. 1 At the close of the eve - ning the watch - es were set. The

2 But now yon - der stars ap - pear in the sky And

3 We shall soon be re - lieved, then drink, drink a - way, then

guards went the round and the ta - ta - ta - too. ta - ta - ta - too.

ta - ra - ra - ra - ra - ra - ra - ra - ra - ra - ra - ra - ra - ra - ra - ra - ra - ra - ra - ra - ra - ra - ra - ra - ra -

drink_____ a - way, then drink,_____

ta - ta - ta - too. ta - ta - ta - too ta - ta - ta - too

ra - ra - ra - ra - ra is sound - ed on high_____

drink,_____ drink a - way; here, here's to you and to you and to

ta - ta - ta - ta - ta - ta - too was beat, the ta - ta - ta - ta - ta - ta - too was beat.

_____ and ta - ra - ra - ra - ta - ra - ra - ra - ra - ra - ra - ra - ra is sound - ed on high.

you, let us drink, let us drink till tis day, let, let us drink till tis day.

Allegretto   Haydn, *Vergebliches Glück*

10.

Es ist um - sonst, daß dir das Glück ge - wo - gen ist, wenn

Es ist um - sonst, daß dir das Glück ge - wo - gen

FINE

du nicht selbst er - kennst wie sehr du___glück - lich bist. Es ist um -

FINE

ist, wenn du nicht selbst er - kennst, wie sehr du___ glück - lich bist. Es

In vain, when fortune is friendly to you, if you don't know yourself how lucky you are.

Haydn, *Thy Voice O Harmony*

Thomas Morley, *Say, Gentle Nymphs*

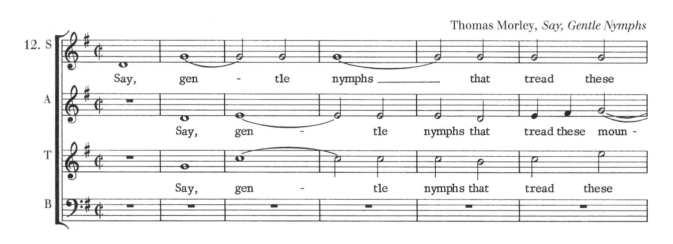

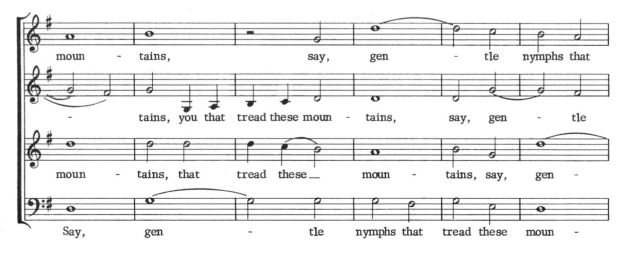

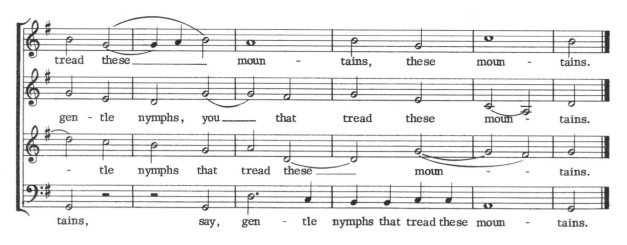

tread these _____ moun - tains, these moun - tains.

gen - tle nymphs, you _____ that tread these moun - tains.

- tle nymphs that tread these _____ moun - tains.

tains, say, gen - tle nymphs that tread these moun - tains.

Mozart, *Heiterkeit und leichtes Blut*

13.

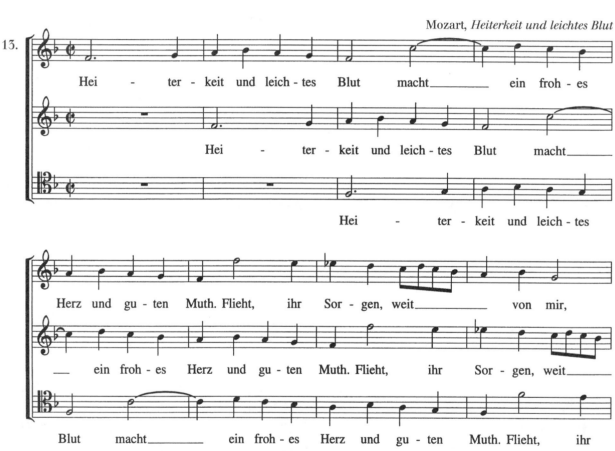

Hei - ter - keit und leich - tes Blut macht _____ ein froh - es

Hei - ter - keit und leich - tes Blut macht _____

Hei - ter - keit und leich - tes

Herz und gu - ten Muth. Flieht, ihr Sor - gen, weit _____ von mir,

__ ein froh - es Herz und gu - ten Muth. Flieht, ihr Sor - gen, weit _____

Blut macht _____ ein froh - es Herz und gu - ten Muth. Flieht, ihr

trübt nicht mei - nes Her - zens Se - - - - - -

___ von mir, trübt nicht mei - nes Her - zens Se -

Sor - gen, weit_____ von mir, trübt nicht mei - nes Her -

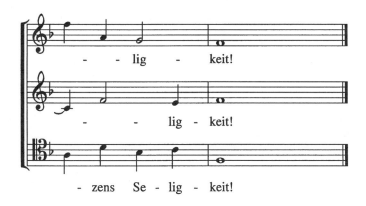

- - lig - keit!

- - lig - keit!

- zens Se - lig - keit!

Happiness and lightheartedness make a merry spirit and a good mood. Fly, cares, away from me, do not disturb my heart's happiness.

Thomas Morley, *Sing We and Chant It*

14. S

Sing we and chant it, While love doth grant it,

S

Sing we and chant it, While love doth grant it,

A

Sing we and chant it, While love doth___ grant it,

T

Sing we and chant it, While love doth grant it,

B

Sing we and chant it, While love doth grant it,

Mozart, *Auf das Wohl aller Freunde*

15.

Here's to all friends. Let's all live well.

M. Ippolitof-Ivanof, *Bless the Lord, O My Soul*

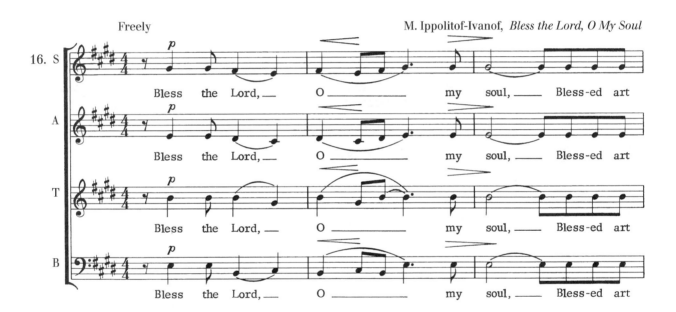

11

Rhythm: Syncopation

Preliminary Exercises

Canons and Duets

Exercises Emphasizing Sixths, Sevenths, and Octaves

Pitch: Other Seventh Chords

Preliminary Exercises

Melodies

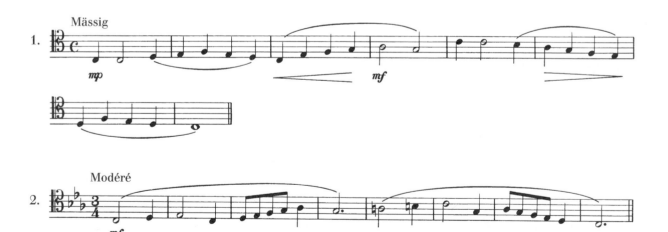

Duets and Trios

124

Part Music

Part II

Common Practice Techniques:
Chromatic

12

Pitch: Decorative Chromaticism

Preliminary Exercises

These exercises introduce chromatically altered nonharmonic tones. For the chromatic syllables, see p. ix.

128

Melodies

Pitch: Inflected Scale Degrees

Preliminary Exercises

For the *solfège* syllables for the chromatic scale, see p. ix.

Pitch: Scalar Variants in Minor

Preliminary Exercises

12.

13.

14.

Melodies

Allegro

1.

f

Espressivo

2.

f

mp

$cresc.$

f

Langsam

3.

p

$rit.$

Fliessend

9.

mp

cresc. poco a poco

rall.

f dim.   *mp*

Canons and Duets

Canon
Comodo

1.

p

mp

p

Lento ostinato

2.

mp

Grazioso

3.

mf

140

4. Dolce

Part Music

1. Solenne

Pitch: Modal Borrowing

Preliminary Exercises

1.

2.

Melodies

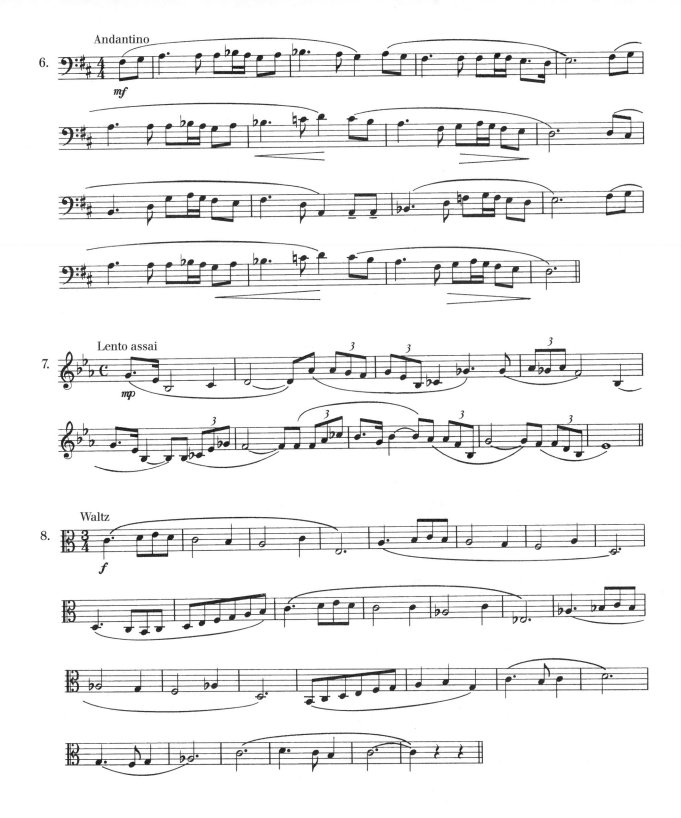

145

146

Duets

Part Music

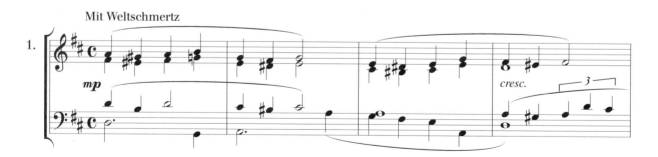

2. Maestoso

13

Music from the Literature

1.

Schop, *Werde munter mein Gemüte*

2.

Bach, *Werde munter mein Gemüte*

3.

Lieblich

Schubert, *Der Morgenstern*

Stern der Lie - be, Glanz - ge - bil - de, glü - hend

Star of love, shimmering image, glowing as heaven's bride, you wander through the realm of light, announcing the dawn.

John Smith, *The Silver Swan*

4. 1 The sil - ver swan, who liv - ing had no

2 Lean - ing her breast a - gainst the reed - y

3 'Fare - well all joys;___ Oh___ death, come close my

note, Till death ap-proach'd un - lock'd her si - lent throat;

shore, Thus sung___ her first and last___ and___ sung no more:

eyes; More geese than swans now live, more fools than wise.'

Allegro   Haydn, *Herr von Gänsewitz*

Be - fehlt doch drau - ßen still zu schwei - gen,   ich muß jetzt mei - nen

Na - men schrei - ben.   Be - fehlt doch drau - ßen still zu schwei - gen,   ich

muß jetzt mei - nen   Na - men schrei - ben,   ich muß, ich muß jetzt mei - nen

Ordered by others to be silent, I now must write my name.

Andante moderato

Brahms, *German Requiem*

7. S: Lord, make me to know, know the mea - sure of my

A: Lord, make me to know, know the mea - sure of my

T: Lord, make me to know, know the mea - sure of my

B: Lord, make me to know, know the mea - sure of my

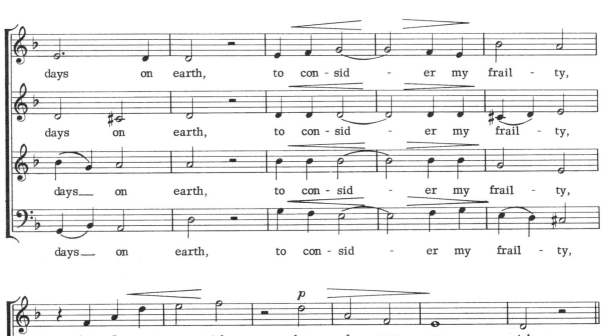

days   on   earth,   to   con - sid   -   er   my   frail   -   ty,

days   on   earth,   to   con - sid   -   er   my   frail   -   ty,

days___ on   earth,   to   con - sid   -   er   my   frail   -   ty,

days___ on   earth,   to   con - sid   -   er   my   frail   -   ty,

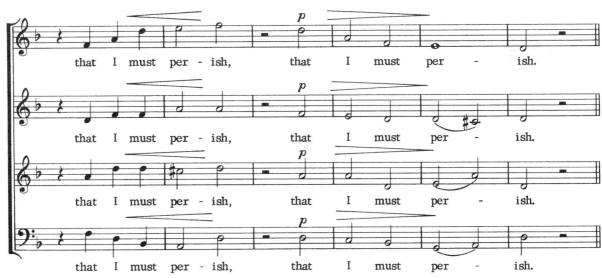

that   I   must   per - ish,   that   I   must   per   -   ish.

that   I   must   per - ish,   that   I   must   per   -   ish.

that   I   must   per - ish,   that   I   must   per   -   ish.

that   I   must   per - ish,   that   I   must   per   -   ish.

14

Pitch: Secondary Dominants

Preliminary Exercises

In preparing these exercises, it will be helpful to first locate and analyze the altered chords.

14.

15.

16.

17.

18.

Melodies

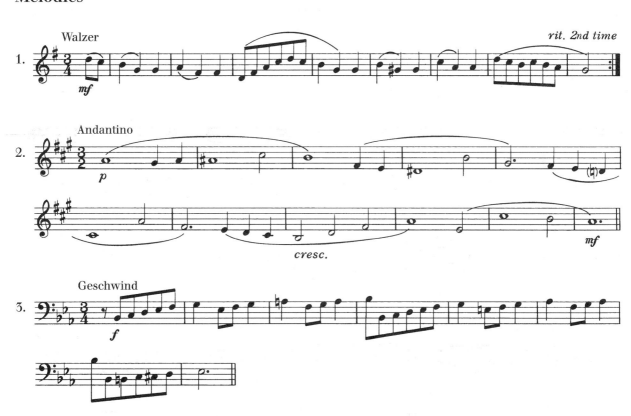

160

Canons and Duets

Morendo

6.

167

15

Pitch: Modulations to Closely Related Keys

Melodies

In preparing these exercises, it will be necessary to determine the keys involved and the
point of modulation. At that point, if the movable *do* system is used, the syllables must be
changed to conform to the new key.

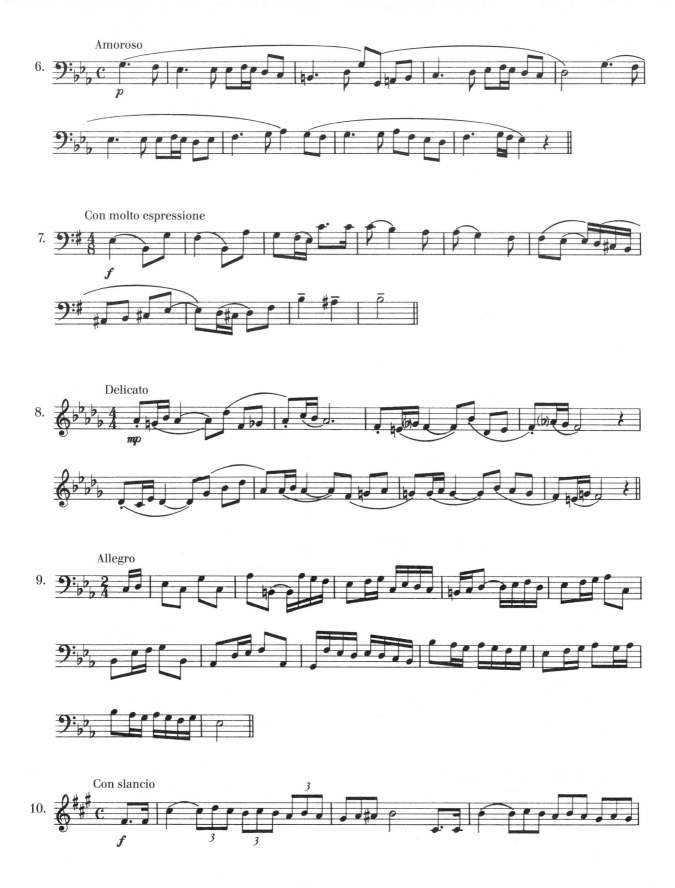

171

172

19. Minuetto

20. Vivace

21. Andante grazioso

173

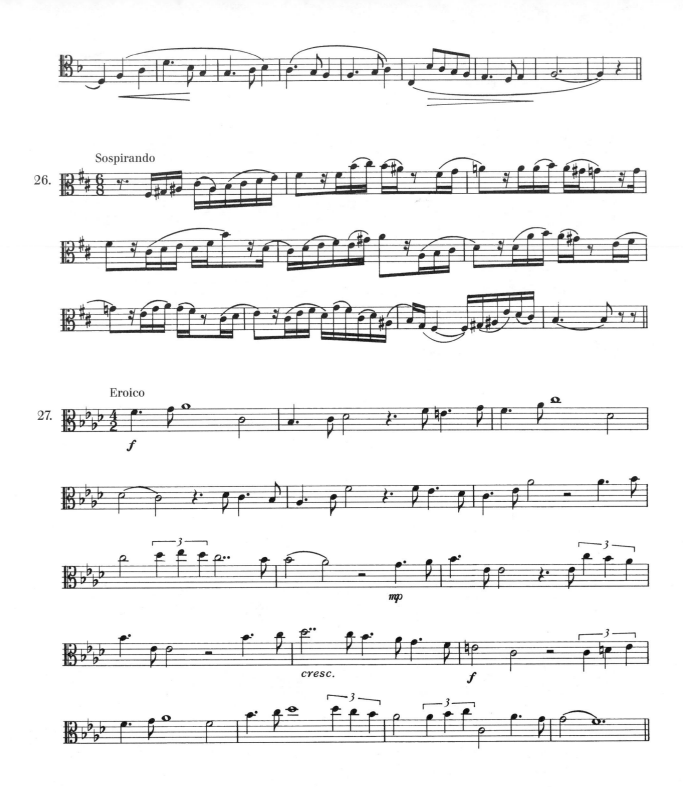

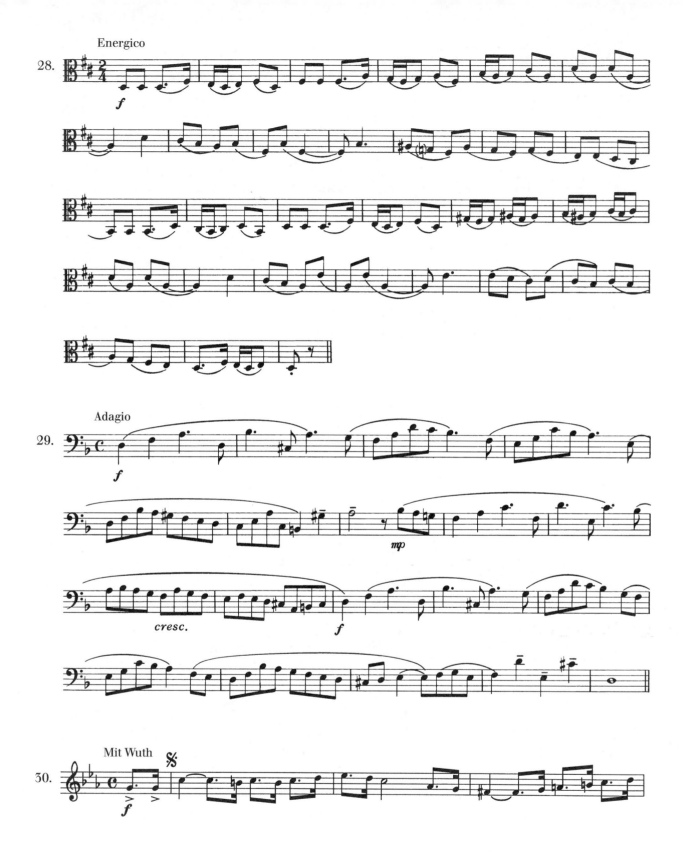

Canons and Part Music

Moderato

Andante contabile

8.

16

Music from the Literature

Beethoven, *Freundschaft*

Mozart, *Ave Maria*

A - ve Ma - ri - a, A - - ve_ Ma - ri - a!

A - - ve, A - - ve_ Ma - ri - a!

A - ve Ma - ri - a, Ma - ri - a, A -

- ve, A - ve Ma - ri - a, A - ve, A - ve!

Be by my side, Narcissus, every morning. My large mirror shall be a home for you.

George Hogarth, *Sound the Clarion!*

Henry Purcell, *Prithee, Ben't So Sad and Serious*

5. 1 Prith-ee, be not so sad and se-ri-ous, Noth-ing's

2 But if bus-i-ness, love, or sor-row, that pos-

3 Let the glass run its round, And each good

got by grief or cares; Mel-an-chol-y's

ses es thus thy mind, bid 'em come a-

fel - low keep his ground; And if there be an - y

too im-pe - ri-ous Where it comes still dom - i - neers.

gain to mor - row, We are now to mirth in - clined.

flinch - er found, We'll have, we'll have his soul new coined.

Poco adagio

Haydn, *Auf einen adeligen Dummkopf*

Das nenn' ich ei - nen E - del - mann: sein Ur - ur - ur - ur - Äl - ter-

Das nenn' ich ei - nen E - del - mann: sein

ahn war äl - ter ei - nen Tag als un - ser al - ler Ahn, war äl - ter ei - nen Tag als__

Ur - ur - ur - ur - Äl - ter - ahn war äl - ter ei - nen Tag als

un - ser al - ler__ Ahn, war äl - ter ei - nen Tag als un - ser al - le

Das nenn' ich ei - nen E - del - mann: sein Ur - ur - ur - ur - Äl - ter-

un - ser__ al - ler Ahn, war äl - ter ei - nen Tag als__ un - ser al - ler__

Ahn, war äl - ter ei - nen Tag_____ als un - ser

That's what I call a nobleman: his great-great-great ancestor was older by one day than any of our ancestors.

Dear, beautiful idol of mine, do not forget me.

glos - - es, hark her love too dis - clo - -

wan - ton glos - - es, hark her love too dis -

- - es too dis - clos - - es, Hark

- clos - - - - - - es, Hark her love

1. her love too dis - clos - es too dis - clos - - es. Where the sweet - es.

2. too dis - clos - es too dis - clos - - - es. - es.

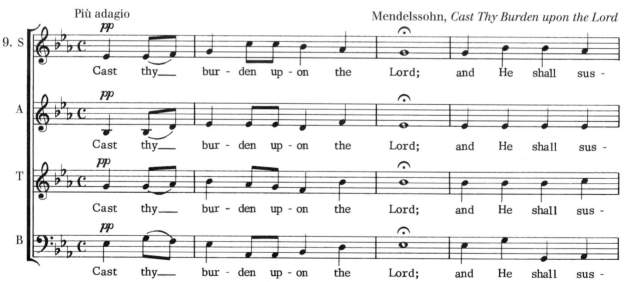

Più adagio

Mendelssohn, *Cast Thy Burden upon the Lord*

9. S Cast thy__ bur - den up - on the Lord; and He shall sus -

A Cast thy__ bur - den up - on the Lord; and He shall sus -

T Cast thy__ bur - den up - on the Lord; and He shall sus -

B Cast thy__ bur - den up - on the Lord; and He shall sus -

tain thee: He never will suf - fer the right-eous to fall; He is at thy

tain thee: He never will suf - fer the right-eous to fall; He is at thy

tain thee: He never will suf - fer the right-eous to fall; He is at thy

tain thee: He never will suf - fer the right-eous to fall; He is at thy

right hand. Thy mer-cy, Lord, is great, and far a - bove the heavens. Let

right hand. Thy mer-cy, Lord, is great, and far a - bove the heavens. Let

right hand. Thy mer-cy, Lord, is great, and far a - bove the heavens. Let

right hand. Thy mer-cy, Lord, is great, and far a - bove the heavens. Let

none be made a - sham - ed that wait up - on Thee!

none be made a - sham - ed that wait up - on Thee!

none be made a - sham - ed that wait up - on Thee!

none be made a - sham - ed that wait up - on Thee!

At one time, C clefs other than Alto clef and Tenor clef were commonly used. Mezzo-soprano clef locates middle C on the second line; Soprano clef locates middle C on the first line. For practice in reading these clefs, here is a Bach chorale with its original clefs.

J. S. Bach, *Was Gott thut, das ist wohlgethan*

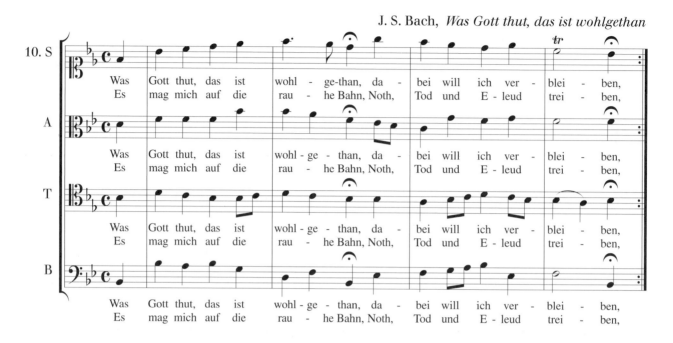

What God does is good; in this opinion I will persist.
Even if my lot is a rough one, (even if it is) need, death, and misery.
God will hold me like a father in his arms–therefore I will let Him rule.

in - fan - cy, Our con - fi - dence and joy shall be, The

in - fan - cy, Our con - fi - dence and joy shall be, The

in - fan - cy, Our con - fi - dence and joy shall be, The

in - fan - cy, Our con - fi - dence and joy shall be, The

pow'r of Sa - tan break - ing, Our peace e - ter - nal mak - ing.

pow'r of Sa - tan break - ing, Our peace e - ter - nal mak - ing.

pow'r of Sa - tan break - ing, Our peace e - ter - nal mak - ing.

pow'r of Sa - tan break - ing, Our peace e - ter - nal mak - ing.

J. S. Bach, *Thee with Tender Care*

12. S

Thee with ten - der care I'll cher - ish; Live to Thee, Die to

A

Thee with ten - der care I'll cher - ish; Live to Thee, Die to

T

Thee with ten - der care I'll cher - ish; Live to Thee, Die to

B

Thee with ten - der care I'll cher - ish; Live to Thee, Die to

Thee: Thus I shall not per - ish, But with Thee a - bide for -
Thee: Thus I shall not per - ish, But with Thee a - bide for -
Thee: Thus I shall not per - ish, But with Thee a - bide for -
Thee: Thus I shall not per - ish, But with Thee a - bide for -

ev - er, Joy - ful - ly, peace - ful - ly, Where life end - eth nev - er.
ev - er, Joy - ful - ly, peace - ful - ly, Where life end - eth nev - er.
ev - er, Joy - ful - ly, peace - ful - ly, Where life end - eth nev - er.
ev - er, Joy - ful - ly, peace - ful - ly, Where life end - eth nev - er.

Etwas langsam   Brahms, *In stiller Nacht*

13. Soprano

In stil - ler Nacht, zur er - sten Wacht, ein Stimm be - gunnt zu

Alto

In stil - ler Nacht, zur er - sten Wacht, ein Stimm be - gunnt zu

Tenor

In stil - ler Nacht, zur er - sten Wacht, ein Stimm be - gunnt zu

Bass

In stil - ler Nacht, zur er - sten Wacht, zu

197

flos - sen, die Blü - me - lein, mit Trä - nen rein hab ich sie all be - gos - sen.

In the still of night, at the first watch, a voice began to lament; the night wind brought me the sweet, soft sound. With bitter pain and sadness my heart was overflowing; I watered the little flowers with my pure tears.

Vivaldi, *Propter magnam gloriam*

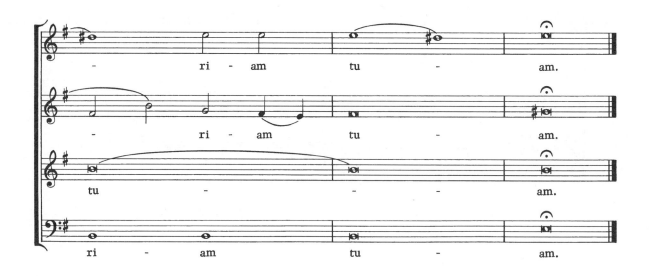

... for thy great glory.

17

Rhythm: Quintuple Meters

Preliminary Exercises

To determine the appropriate conducting pattern, analyze these examples to determine the subdivisions of the measure. For conducting patterns, see Suggestions to the Student, pp. vii–x.

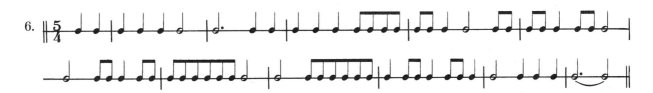

8.
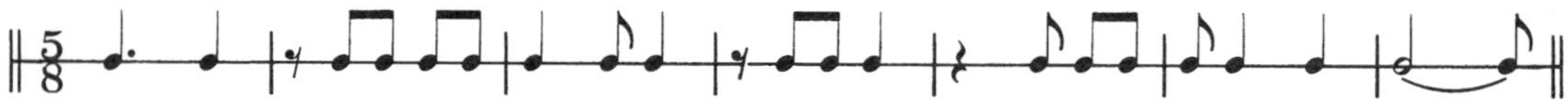

9.
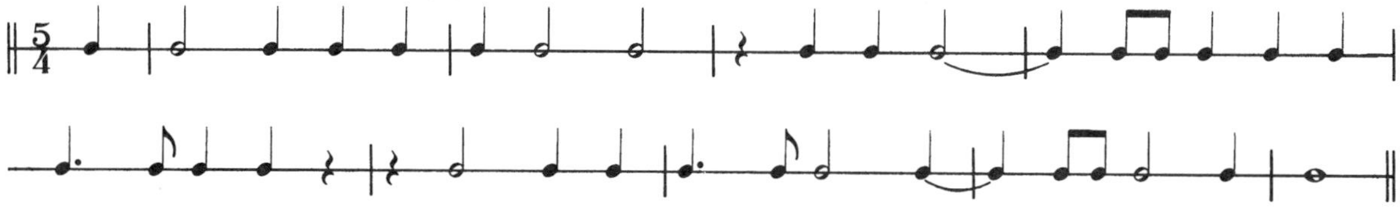

10.
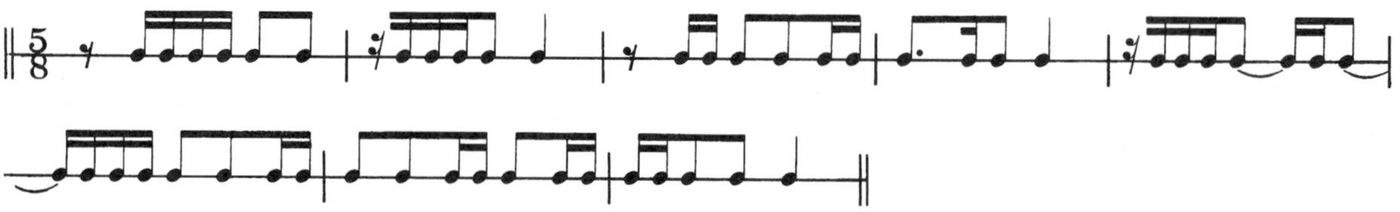

11.
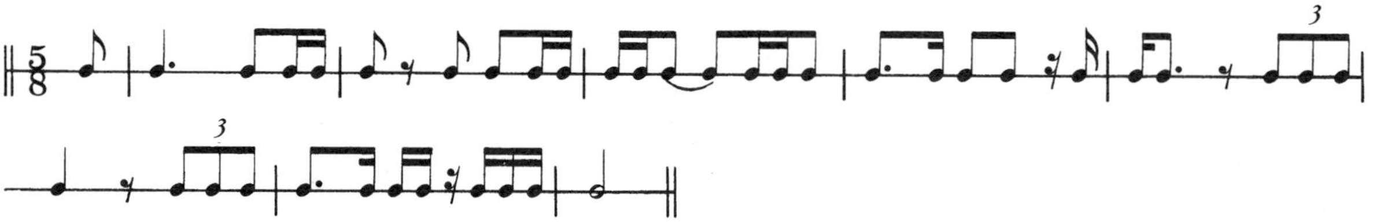

12.
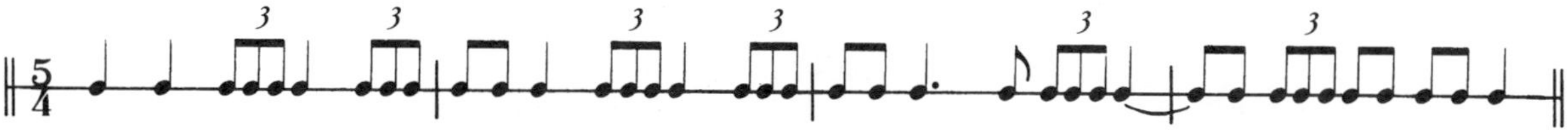

13.
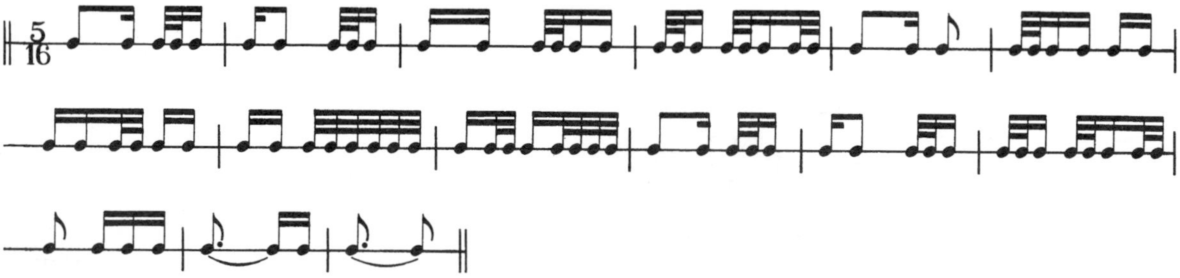

14.
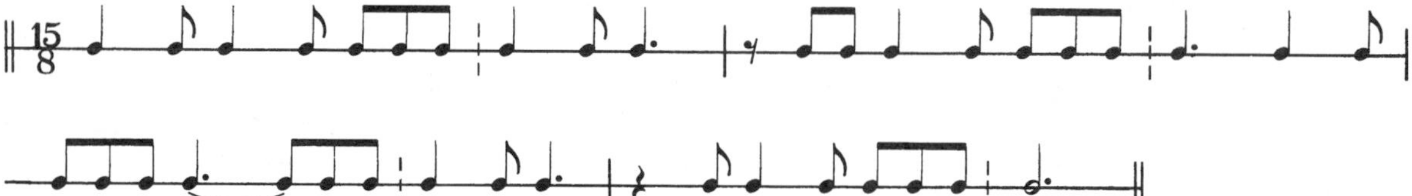

Canons and Duets

Pitch: Chromaticism Implying Altered Chords;
Modulation to Distantly Related Keys

Melodies

26. Leggiero

Part Music

Con forza

2.

Breit und feierlich

3.

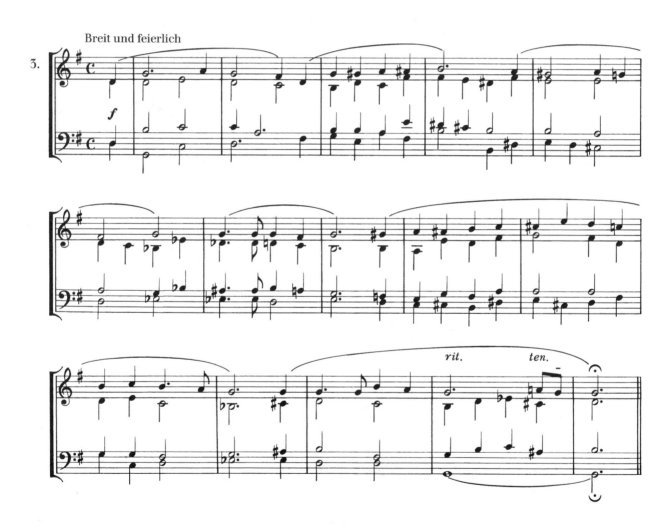

rit.   *ten.*

216

Sehr ausdrucksvoll

4.

18

Music from the Literature

Here lies Hans with his wife. Hans was a cuckold; what then was his wife?

1st version
(Adagio)

Haydn, *Das böse Weib*

Ein ein - zig bö - ses Weib lebt höch - stens in der Welt, nur schlimm, daß je - der

sein's für die - ses einz' - ge hält. Ein ein - zig bö - ses

Ein ein - zig bö - ses Weib lebt

höch - stens in der Welt, nur schlimm, daß je - der sein's für die - ses einz' - ge

Weib ein bö - ses Weib lebt höch - stens, lebt höch - stens in der

Ein ein - zig bö - ses Weib lebt höch - stens in der

hält. Ein ein - zig bö - ses Weib, ein

Welt, nur schlimm, daß je - der, schlimm, daß

2nd version

A singularly wicked wife lives grandly in the world. What a shame that every man deems his wife to be this singular lady.

Mendelssohn, *Elijah*, "Yet Doth the Lord"

He was crucified for us under Pontius Pilate, suffered, and was buried.

Mendelssohn, *Elijah*, "Thanks Be to God"

5.

The stor-my bil-lows are high, their fu-ry is might-y:

But the Lord is

Schubert, *Mass in E♭ Major*, "Benedictus"

Blessed is he who cometh in the name of The Lord.

J. S. Bach, *Chorale*, "Es ist genug"

It is enough! Lord, if it please Thee to make me depart. My Jesus comes. Now good night, oh world. I go to my heavenly home. I surely go there with joy. My great sorrow remains below. It is enough, it is enough!

J. S. Bach, *Chorale,* "Christus, der uns selig macht"

230

Christ, who makes us blessed, who has done no wrong, who was taken for us like a thief in the night, led before a Godless people and falsely accused, laughed at, scorned and spit upon, according to the Scriptures.

Andante

Gluck, *Orfeo*, "Le Porte Stridano"

10.

Le por-te stri-da-no su' ne-ri car-di-ni, e il pas-so

Le por-te stri-da-no su' ne-ri car-di-ni, e il pas-so

Le por-te stri-da-no su' ne-ri car-di-ni, e il pas-so

Le por-te stri-da-no su' ne-ri car-di-ni, e il pas-so

Andante

la - sci-no si - cu - ro e li - be-ro al vin - ci - tor!

la - sci-no si - cu - ro e li - be-ro al vin - ci - tor!

la - sci-no si - cu - ro e li - be-ro al vin - ci - tor!

la - sci-no si - cu - ro e li - be-ro al vin - ci - tor!

Allegro

Le por - te stri - da-no su' ne - ri car - di-ni, e il pas - so

Le por - te stri - da-no su' ne - ri car - di-ni, e il pas - so

Le por - te stri - da-no su' ne - ri car - di-ni, e il pas - so

Le por - te stri - da-no su' ne - ri car - di-ni, e il pas - so

Allegro

236

Let the doors, squealing on black hinges, surely and freely give passage to the victor!

Wagner, *Chorus of the Elder Pilgrims*

der du des Pil - gers Hoff - nung __ bist!

ritard.
dim. *p* *f*

Ge - lobt sei, Jung frau __ süss und __ rein!

ritard.
dim. *p* *p cresc.*

Der Wall __ fahrt wol - le gün - stig __ sein!

f *ritard.*
dim. *p* *f*

Ach, schwer drückt mich der Sün - den Last, kann län - ger sie nicht mehr er - tra - gen: drum will ich auch nicht Ruh' noch Rast, und wäh - le gern mir

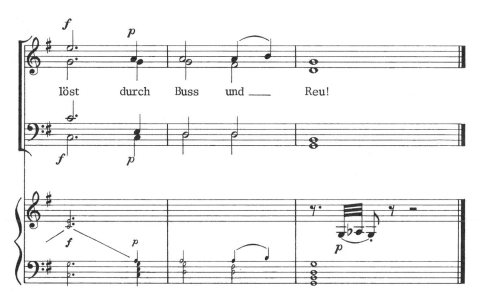

I make my pilgrimage to Thee
O God, Who art the pilgrim's hope!
Praised be the Virgin, sweet and pure!
Be gracious to the pilgrimage.

The burden of sin heavily weighs me down;
I can no longer bear it.
Thus I wish no rest
    and gladly choose toil and pain.
At the high festival of Grace
    I shall humbly pay for my guilt.
Blest be he who is true to his faith,
He shall be saved through penance.

und mir ist, als würd ich wie – der all der ir – ren Qua – len

und mir ist, als würd ich wie – der all der ir – ren Qua – len

und mir ist, als würd ich wie – der all der ir – ren Qua – len

und mir ist, als würd ich wie – der all der ir – ren Qua – len

los, all der ir – – ren Qua – len los.

los, all der ir – ren Qua – len los.

los, all der ir – ren Qua – len los.

los, der Qua – – len los.

Thou wondrously cool forest night,
    I greet you a thousand times.
After the loudness of the troubled world,
    how sweet is your rustling.
Dreamily I lay my tired limbs
    softly on the mossy ground.
And it seems that I have once again
    become free of all my troubles.

pas - sum, im - mo - la - tum in cru - - ce pro ho - mi -

pas - sum, im - mo - la - tum in cru - ce pro ho - mi -

pas - sum, im - mo - la - tum in cru - ce pro ho - mi -

pas - sum, im - mo - la - tum in cru - ce pro ho - mi -

ne: Cu - jus la - tus

ne: Cu - jus la - tus

ne: Cu - jus la - tus

ne: Cu - jus la - tus

per - fo - ra - tum flu - xit a - qua et san - gui - ne:

per - fo - ra - tum flu - xit a - qua et san - gui - ne:

per - fo - ra - tum flu - xit a - qua et san - gui - ne:

per - fo - ra - tum flu - xit a - qua et san - gui - ne:

E - sto no - bis_ prae - gu - sta - tum_ mor - - tis in ex-

E - sto no - bis_ prae - gu - sta - tum_ mor - - tis in ex-

E - sto no - bis_ prae - gu - sta - tum_ mor - tis in

E - sto no - bis_ prae - gu - sta - tum_ mor - tis in

Hail holy body, born of The Virgin Mary, truly having suffered, sacrificed on the cross for man, whose pierced side flowed with water and blood: be for us a foretaste in the trial of death.

Glory to God in the highest.

Part III

Twentieth-Century Techniques

19

Rhythm: Irregular Meters

Preliminary Exercises

6. 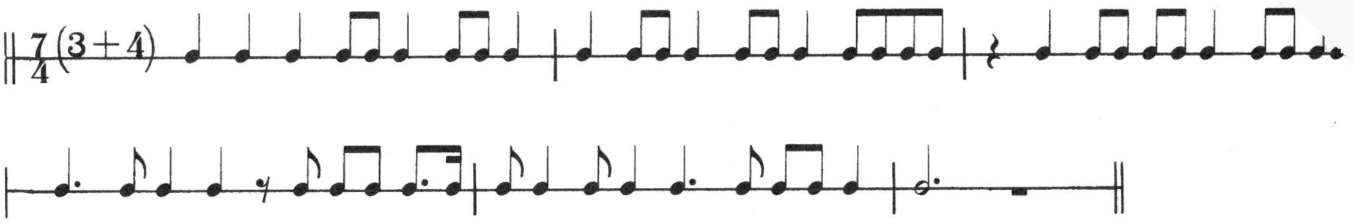

7. 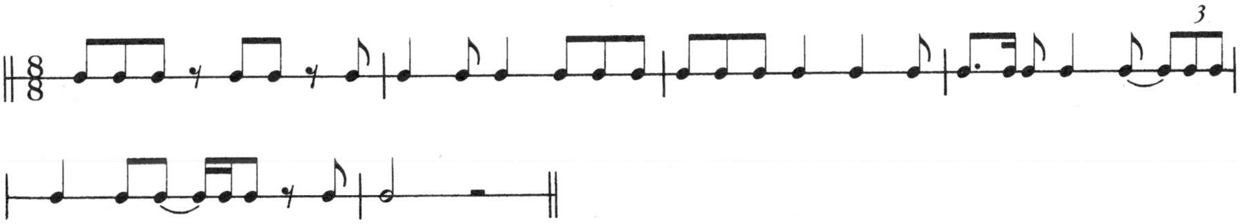

8. 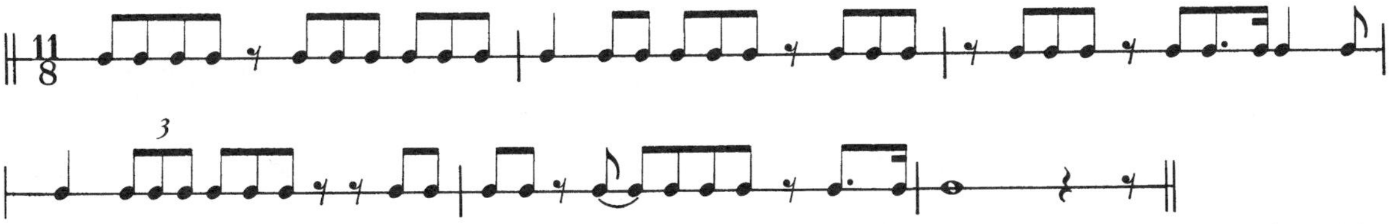

9. 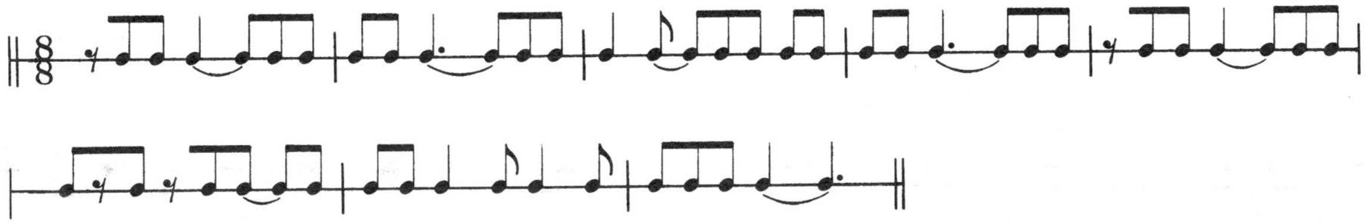

10. 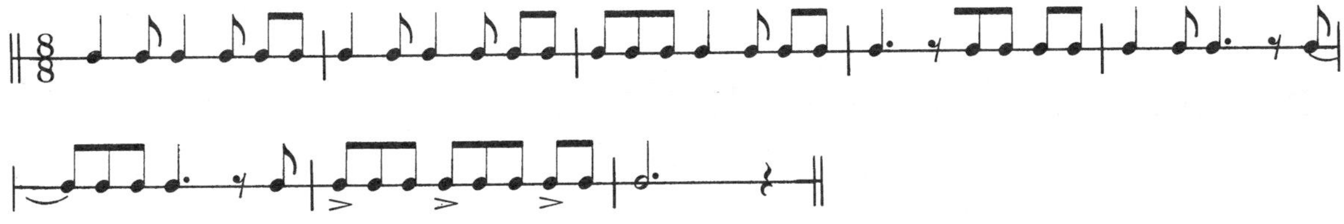

11. 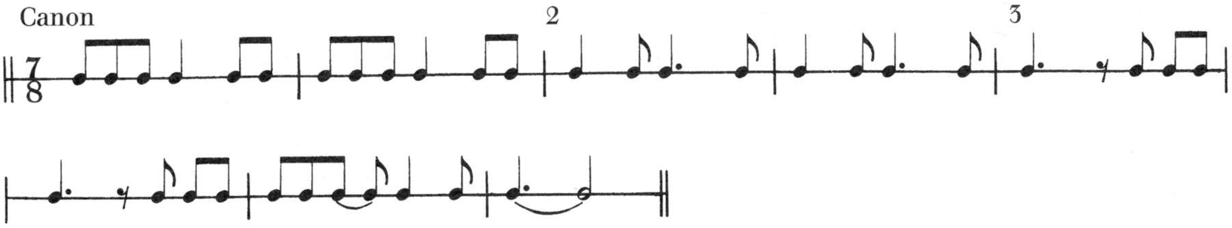

...tonic Modes

Exercises

...al music, one may determine the syllable name for the tonic note from the ...or example, *mi* would be the name of the tonic note in Phrygian mode, and ...e name of the tonic note in Myxolydian mode.

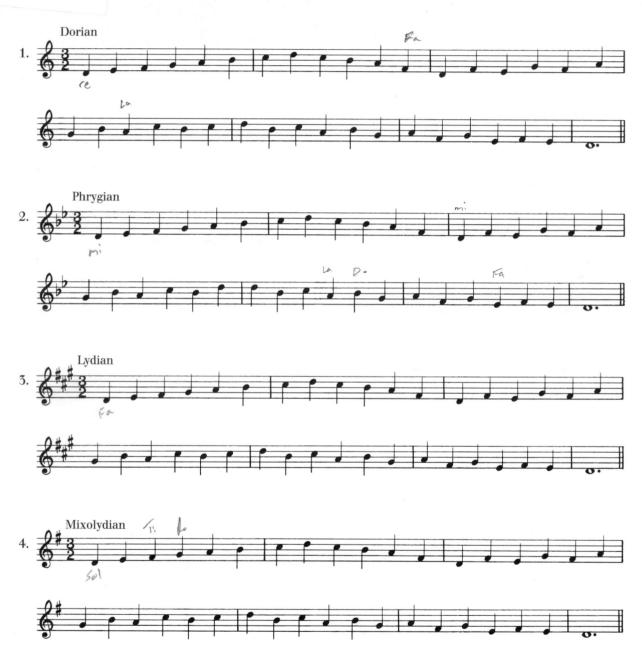

258

Pitch: Changing Clefs

Melodies with Changing Clefs

Melodies

262

Andante semplice

21.

Avec mouvement

22.

23. Con forza

Part Music

Shalom

With motion

Sha - lom, sha - lom, ____ sha - lom, ____ sha -

Sha - lom, ____ sha - lom, ____ sha - lom, ____ sha -

Sha - lom, ____ sha - lom, sha - lom, ____

Sha - lom, sha - lom, sha - lom _____ sha -

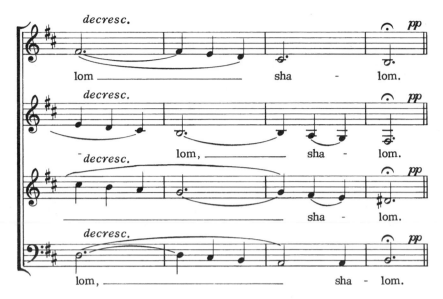

lom _____ sha - lom.

lom, _____ sha - lom.

sha - lom.

lom, _____ sha - lom.

Peace.

Smoothly

Dona nobis pacem

2.

mp

Do - na no - bis pa - - cem. _____ Do - -

mp *mf*

Do - na, Do - na

mp

Do - - - -

mf

Do - na no - bis

- na _____ no - bis pa - - cem. _____ Do - na -

mp

no - bis ___ pa - - cem. Do - - - - -

na no - - - - - - - - bis

pa - cem.

no - bis pa - cem.

- na no - bis pa - cem.

pa - cem, pa - cem.

Give us peace.

Accompanied Canon
Slowly and smoothly

3.

20

Rhythm: Changing Meters

Preliminary Exercises

1.

2.

3.

4.

5.

6.

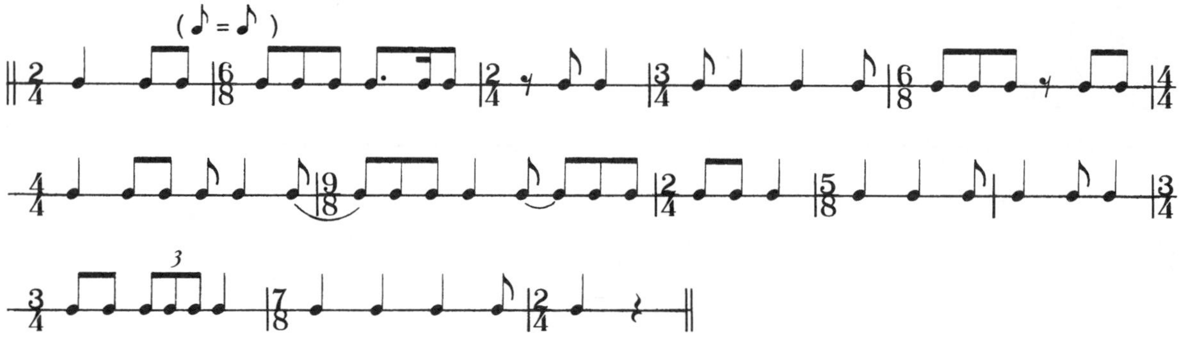

7.

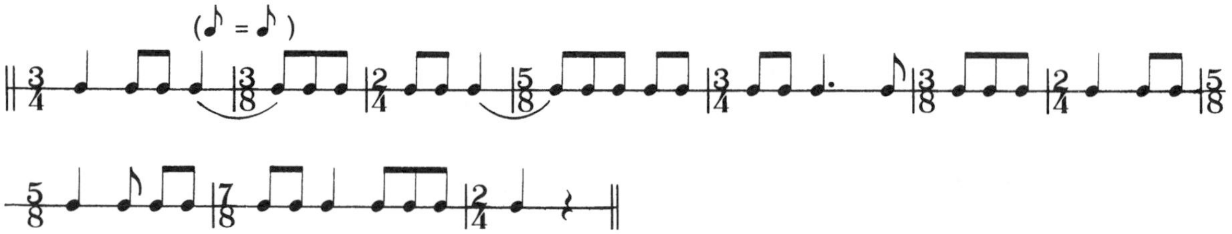

8.

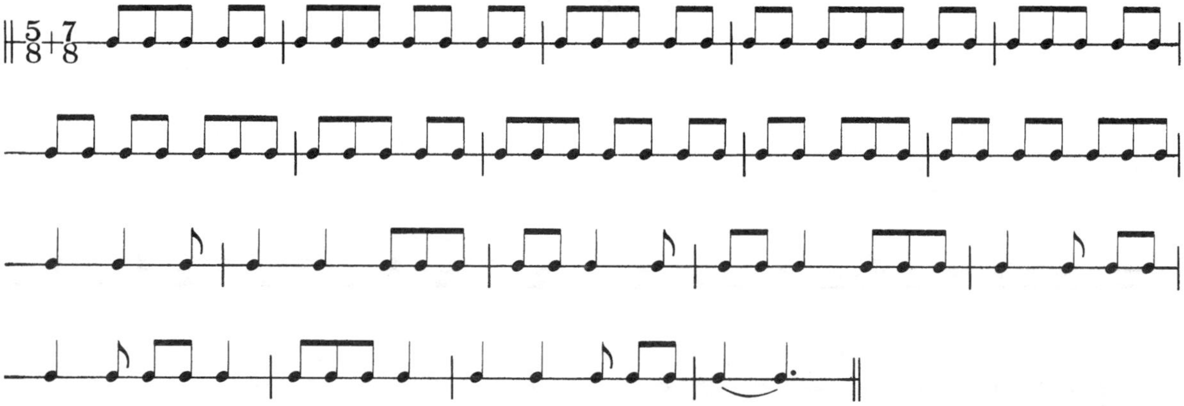

9.

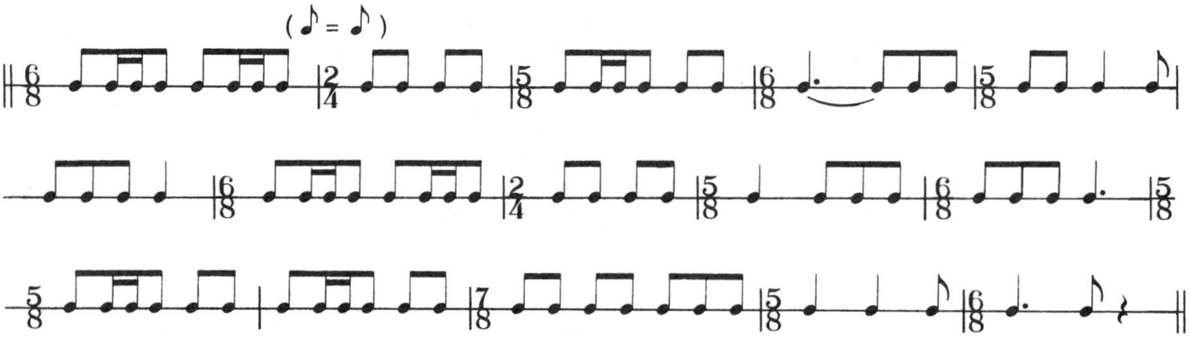

Pitch: Pandiatonicism

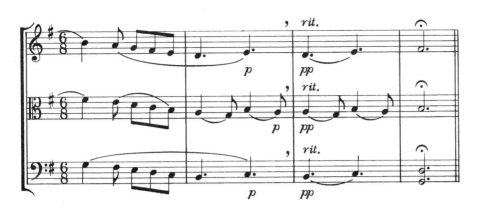

6.

7.

275

The Place Where We Meet

11. The place where we meet to seek the high- est is
The place where we meet to seek the high- est is
The place where we meet to seek the high- est is
The place where we meet to seek the high- est is

ho - - - - ly ground.

ho - - - - ly ground

ho - - - - ly ground.

ho - - - - ly ground.

Praise God

12.

Praise__ God, praise_____ God, praise_____

Praise__ God, praise_____ God, praise _____

Praise__ God, praise_____ God, praise_____

Praise__ God, praise_____ God, praise_____

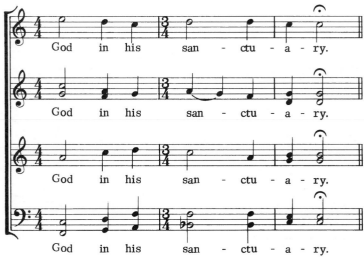

God in his san - ctu - a - ry.

God in his san - ctu - a - ry.

God in his san - ctu - a - ry.

God in his san - ctu - a - ry.

Fairly slow

14.

Al - le-lu - ia, al - le-lu - ia, al - le-lu - - - - ia, al - le-lu - - - - ia, A - men.

Al - le-lu - ia, al - le-lu - ia, al - le-lu - - - - ia, al - le-lu - - - ia, A - men.

Al - le-lu - ia, al - le-lu - ia, al - le-lu - - - - ia, al - le - - lu - - - - ia, A - men.

Al - le-lu - ia, al - le-lu - ia, al - le-lu - - - - ia, al - le-lu - - - ia, A - men.

21

Rhythm: Syncopation Including
Irregular and Mixed Meters

Preliminary Exercises

6.

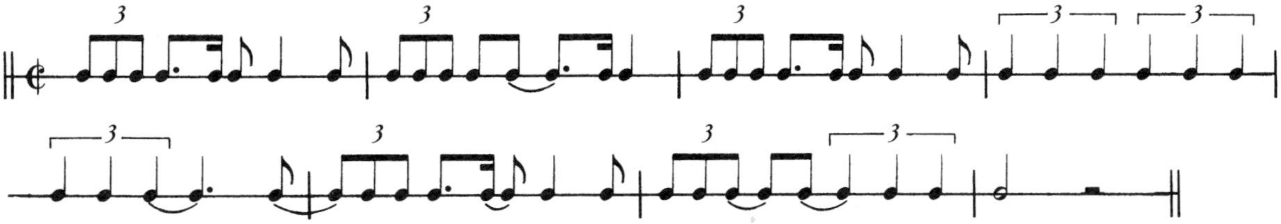

7.

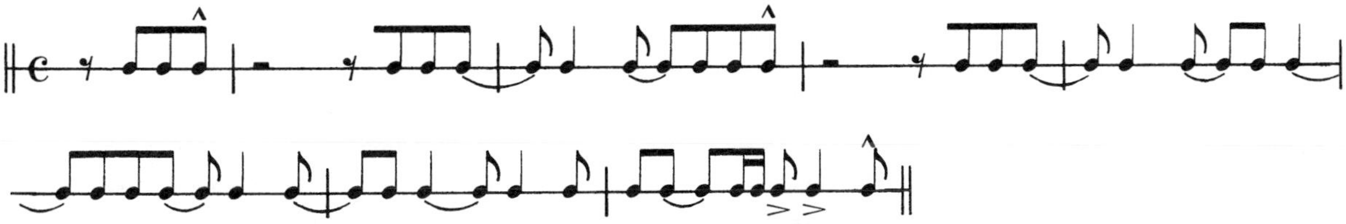

8.

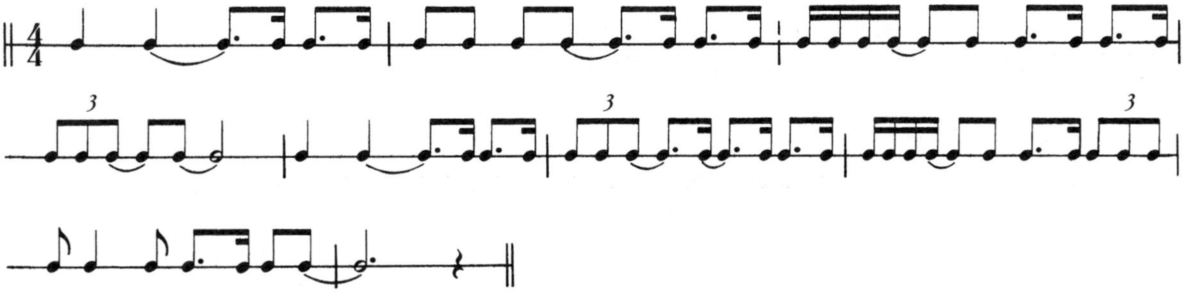

9.

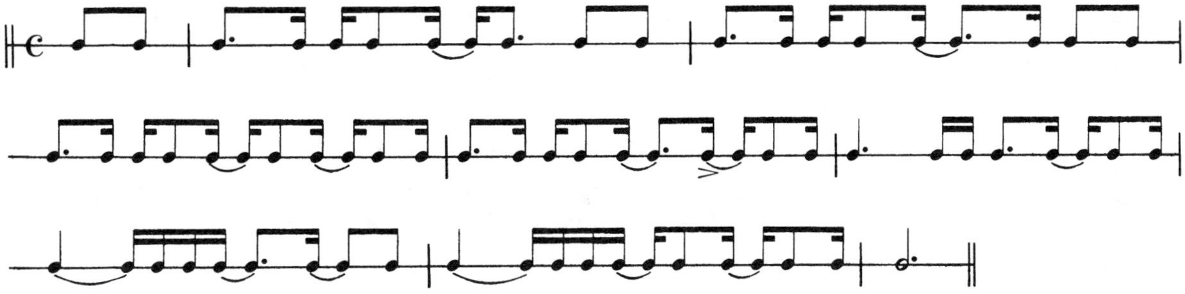

10.

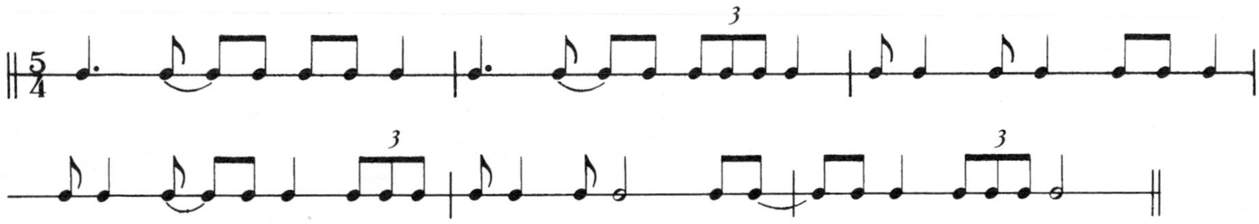

Pitch: Extended and Altered Tertian Harmony

Preliminary Exercises

Analyzing these exercises for harmonic content and melodic pattern before singing them will be helpful.

    Possible strategies for hearing and singing are:

1. Using *fixed do* without inflected syllables.

2. Using *fixed do* with inflected syllables.

3. Using *movable do* locally for rapidly moving chordal or scalar patterns, as in exercises 8 ff.

4. Using a neutral syllable.

Melodies

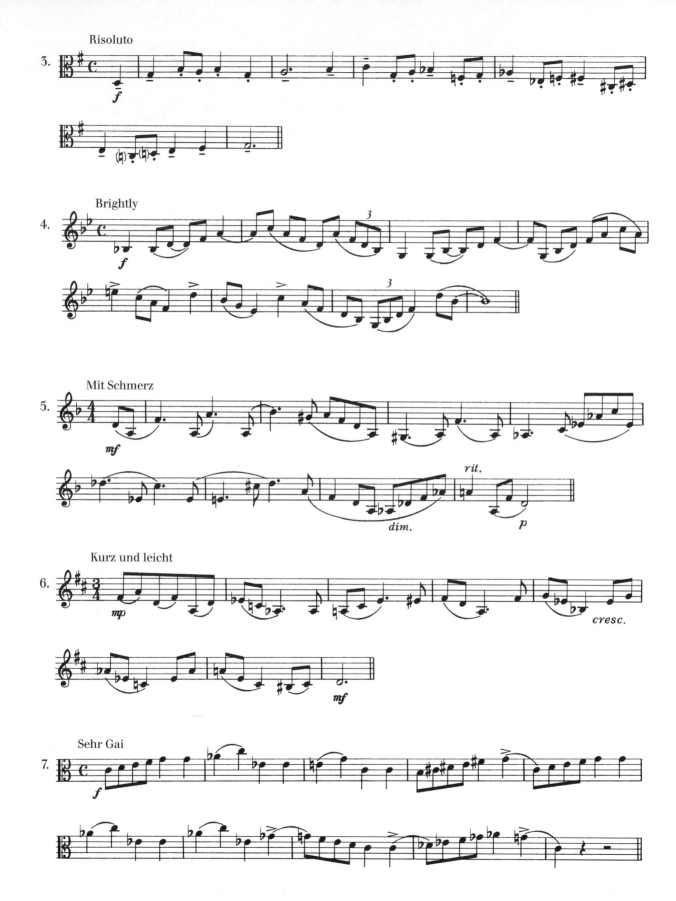

11. **Avec mouvement**

12. **Dolce**

Performance directions: Very distant and pure tone; blend and balance with care; no vibrato; observe dynamics carefully. All attacks and releases cued by the conductor.

Note and rest values:

o ⌐·⌐ = very long   ρ ⋏ = long   ρ ⌒ = shorter   ρ , = shortest

22

Pitch: Exotic Scales

Preliminary Exercises

Analyzing these exercises for tonal center (if any), scalar types, and melodic patterns will be helpful.

293

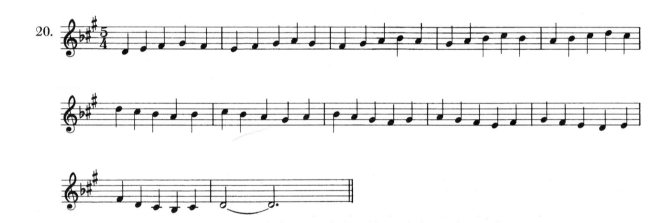

Melodies

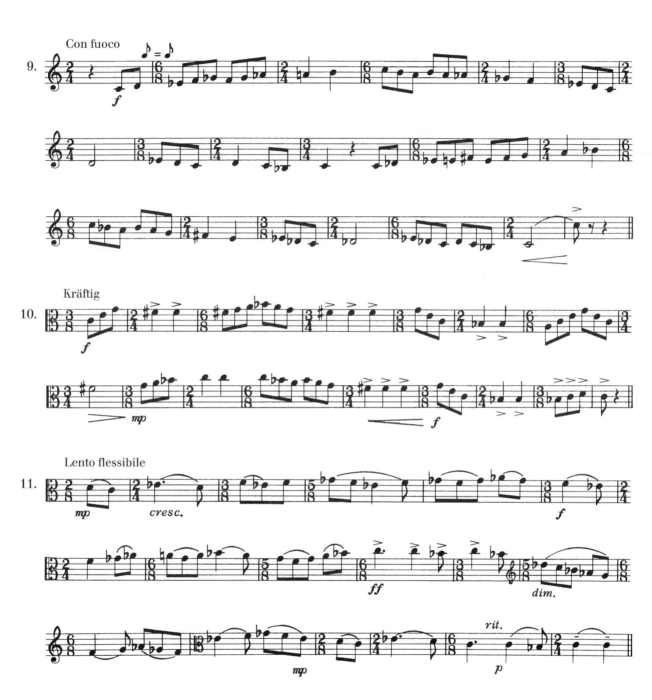

Duets

23

Rhythm: Complex Divisions of the Beat

Preliminary Exercises

7.

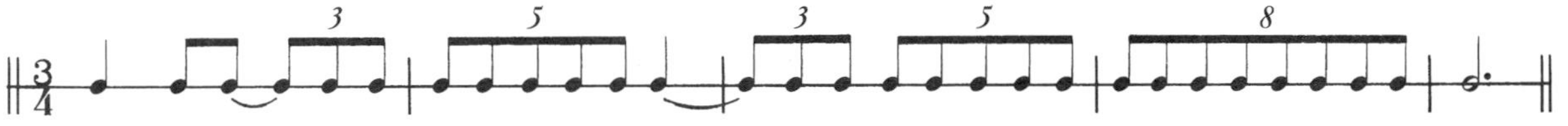

8.

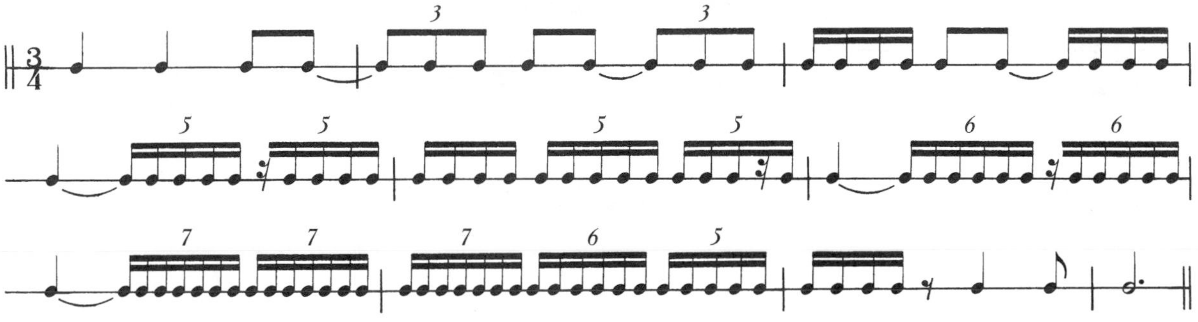

9.

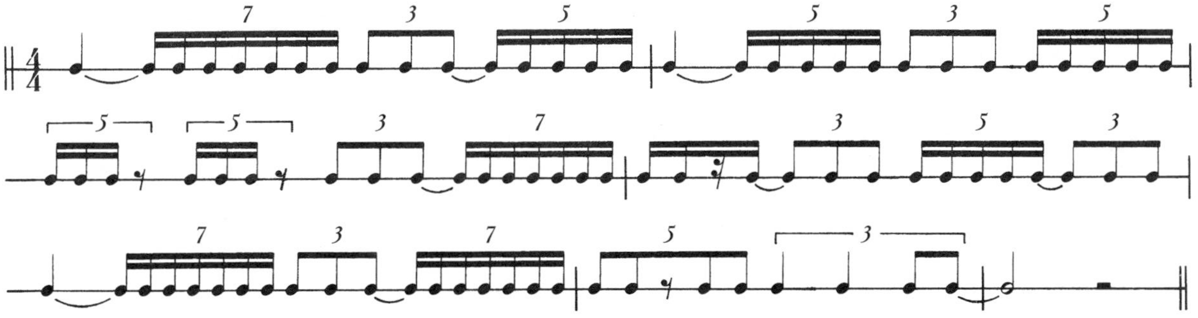

10.

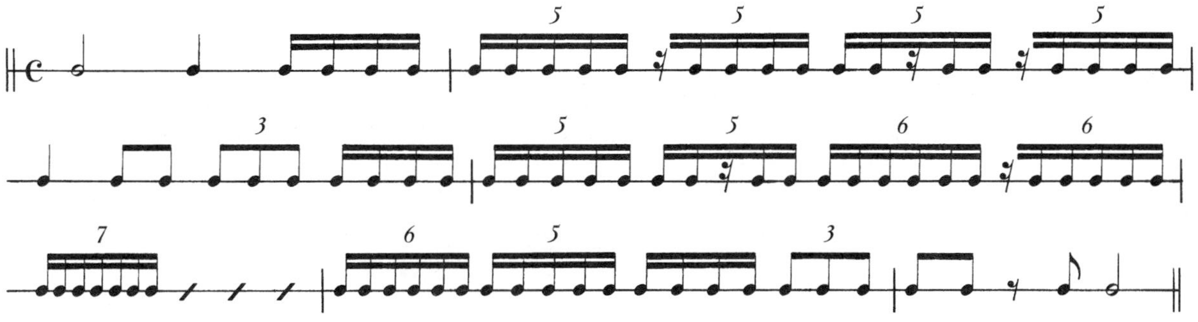

11.

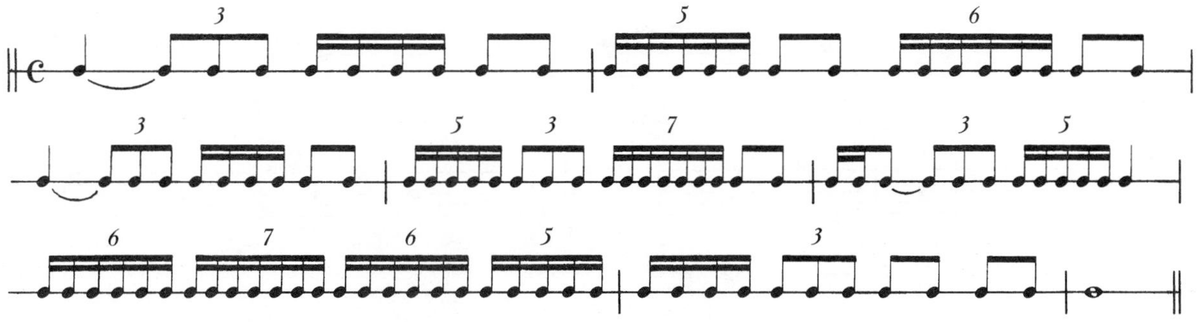

Pitch: Quartal Harmony

Preliminary Exercises

305

10.

11.

12.

13.

Melodies

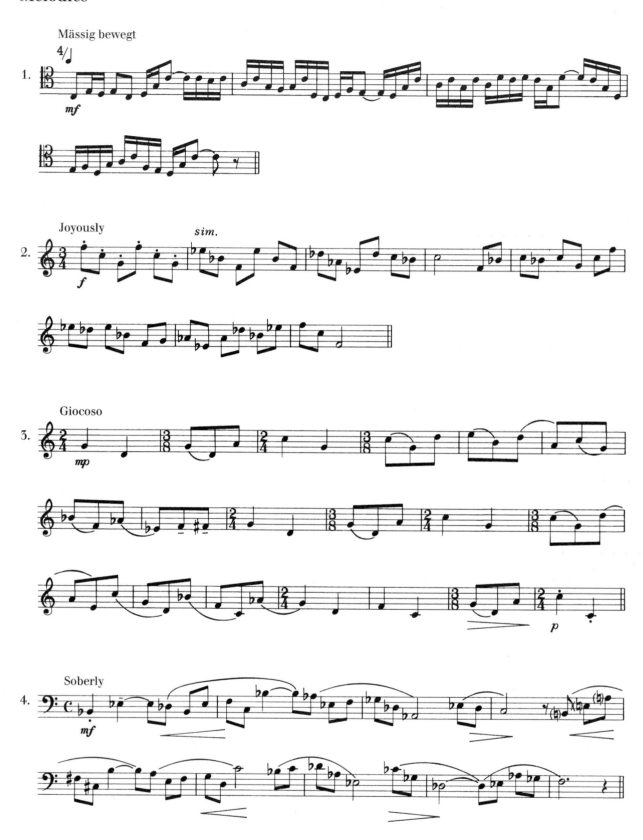

Appassionato e molto espressivo

13.

Part Music

Austerely

1.

Grazioso

2.

313

Mässig

5.

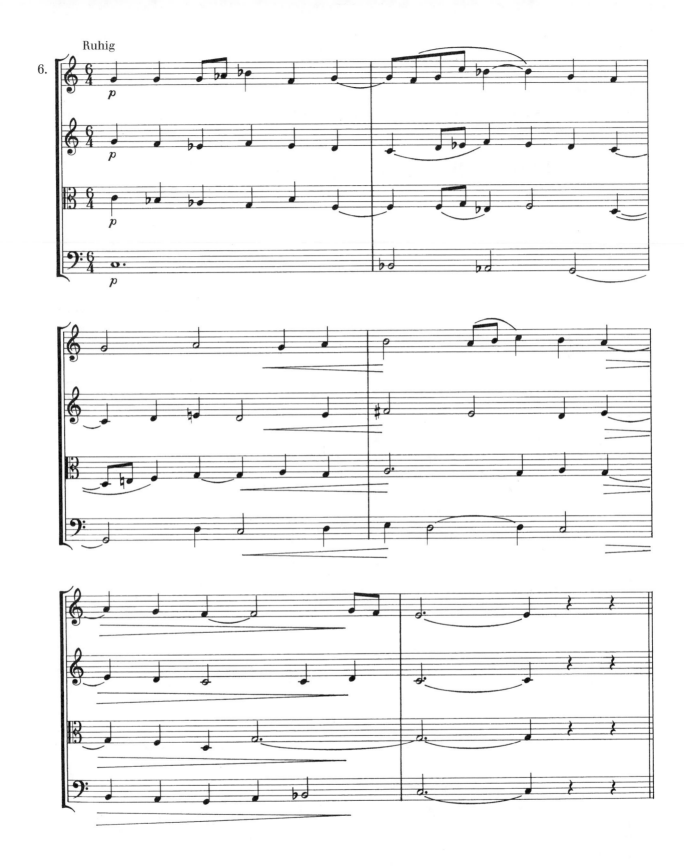

24

Rhythm: Polyrhythms and Polymeters

Preliminary Exercises

317

Pitch: Polyharmony and Polytonality

Part Music

Andante grazioso

2.

Pesante

3.

321

Allegro gioioso

6.

Molto cantabile

7.

8.

Peace be with you, _____ and with your spir - it,

Peace be with you, _____ and with your spir - it,

May peace be with you, _____ and with your spir - it,

May peace be with you, _____ and with your spir - it,

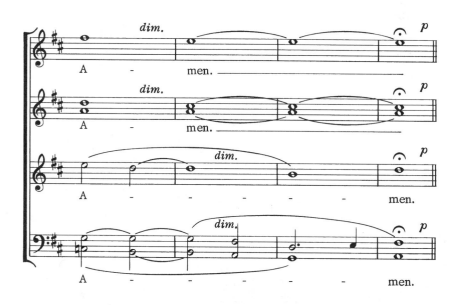

A - men. _____

A - men. _____

A - - - - - men.

A - - - - - men.

Firmly, not too fast

9.

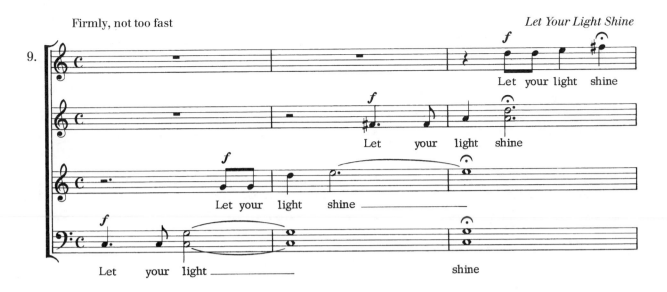

Let your light shine

Let your light shine

Let your light shine _____

Let your light _____ shine

be - fore all peo - ple.

be - fore all peo - ple.

be - fore all peo - ple.

be - fore all peo - ple.

Slow, hushed   *Amen!*

10.

326

Brillante

11.

25

Pitch: Interval Music

Preliminary Exercises

Analyzing these exercises for linear tendencies and melodic and interval patterning will be helpful. Try to retain recurring pitches as reference points. These will often be first and last pitches or the principal pitch of any given segment.

1.

2.

3.

4.

331

Melodies

Mässig

9.

Mit gross schwerigheit

10.

Duets

Night music

1.

26

Serial Music

27

Music from the Literature

The following choral pieces are suggested for sight-reading and ensemble performance in class. They represent a broad survey of techniques and materials found in twentieth-century music. They are listed in the order in which the materials are presented in Part III.

Trois Chansons, Claude Debussy
Silence and Music, Ralph Vaughn Williams
Hymn to St. Cecilia, Benjamin Britten
Rejoice in the Lamb, Benjamin Britten
Singet den Herrn, Hugo Distler
Four Slavonic Folk Songs, Béla Bartók
Reincarnations, Samuel Barber
Carols of Death, William Schuman
Six Chansons, Paul Hindemith
Mass, Vincent Persichetti

Psalm 67, Charles Ives
Ave Maria, Igor Stravinsky
O sacrum convivium!, Olivier Messiaen
Anthem, The Dove Descending, Igor Stravinsky
Friede auf Erden, Arnold Schoenberg
De Profundis, Arnold Schoenberg
Easter Cantata, Daniel Pinkham
Te Deum, Krzysztof Penderecki
Lux Aeterna, Györgi Ligeti

Glossary

Accelerando (Accel.) (It.) becoming faster
Adagietto (It.) see *Tempo*
Adagio (It.) see *Tempo*
Agile (Fr.) agile, nimble
A la, Alla in the style or manner of
Allegretto (It.) see *Tempo*
Allegro (It.) see *Tempo*
Amabile (It.) amiable, graceful
Amore (It.) love
  Con amore with tenderness
Amoroso (It.) tender and affectionate
Andante (It.) see *Tempo*
Andantino (It.) see *Tempo*
Anima (It.), *Con anima* with life and animation, alt. soulful
Animato (It.), *Animé* (Fr.) animated, with life or spirit
Appassionato (It.) passionately, with intense emotion
Assai (It.) very, extremely, much
Assez (Fr.) enough, sufficiently
Ausdrucksvoll (Ger.) expressively
Avec (Fr.) with

Ballabile (It.) in the style of a dance
Barbaro (It.) barbarous, primitive
Barcarolle (Fr.) boat song
Ben (It.) much
Bien (Fr.) well, good
Bewegt (Ger.) with movement
Breit (Ger.) broad
Brillante (It.) bright, brilliant
Brio (It.) vigor, animation, spirit
Buffo (It.) in a comic style

Calando (It.) gradually softer and slower
Calmo (It.) calm, tranquil
Calore (It.) warmth, animation
Cantabile (It.) in a singing or lyrical style
Comodo (It.) easy, agreeable, comfortable
Con (It.) with

Da capo (D.C.) (It.) repeat from the beginning

D.C. al Fine repeat from the beginning and play to the ending (*Fine*)
Dal Segno (D.S.) (It.) Repeat from the sign (𝄋)
Deciso (It.) boldly, decisively
Deliberatamente (It.) deliberately
Delicato (It.) delicate
Desto (It.) brisk, sprightly
Détaché (Fr.) detached, non legato
Dolce (It.) sweetly, softly
Dolore (It.) grief, sorrow
Doloroso (It.) sorrowfully, sadly

E, et and
Ecclesiastico (It.) of the church
  Nel modo ecclesiastico in the manner of church music
Edel (Ger.) noble
Einfach (Ger.) simple
En allant (Fr.) with movement
Energico (It.) energetic
Erhaben (Ger.) sublime, in a lofty and exalted style
Ernste (Ger.) serious, earnest, gravely

341

Eroico (It.)   heroic
Espressione (It.)   expression, feeling
Espressivo (It.)   expressive
Etwas (Ger.)   somewhat

Feierlich (Ger.)   solemn, festive
Fine (It.)   the end
Flessibile (It.)   flexible, pliant
Fliessend (Ger.)   flowing
Fort (Fr.)   strong
Forza (It.)   force, strength, power
Fröhlich (Ger.)   joyous, happy
Fuoco (It.)   fire
    Con fuoco   with energy or passion
Furioso (It.)   furious

Gai (Fr.)   gay, merry
Geist (Ger.)   spirit
    Mit Geist   with soul or sentiment
Gemütlich (Ger.)   agreeable, genial
Gesangvoll (Ger.)   lyrical
Geschleift (Ger.)   legato, connected
Geschwind (Ger.)   quick, rapid
Giochévole (It.)   merry, sportive
Giocoso, Giojoso (It.)   humorous, jocose
Giusto (It.)   steady, exact, alt. moderate
Gondellied (Ger.)   boat song
Gracieux, Gracieusement (Fr.), *Grazioso* (It.)   graceful
Grave (It.)   see *Tempo*
Gross (Ger.)   great amount, large

Heftig (Ger.)   vehement, boisterous
Hurtig (Ger.)   quick, swiftly

Incalzando (It.)   getting faster and louder
Innig (Ger.)   sincerely, with depth of feeling
Innocente (It.)   innocently

Jolie (Fr.)   pleasant, pretty

Keck (Ger.)   pert, fearless, bold
Klar (Ger.)   clear, bright
Klingend (Ger.)   sonorous, ringing
Kraft (Ger.)   strength, power
Kräftig (Ger.)   powerfully, vigorously
Kurz (Ger.)   short, detached, staccato

Ländler (Ger.)   country dance, in a rustic and popular style
Langsam (Ger.)   slow
Larghetto (It.)   see *Tempo*
Largo (It.)   see *Tempo*
Lebhaft (Ger.)   lively
Legato (It.)   connected, smoothly
Leggiero (It.)   light, delicate
Leicht (Ger.)   lightly
Lentamente (It.), *Lentement* (Fr.)   slowly
Lento (It.), *Lent* (Fr.)   see *Tempo*
Liscio (It.)   simple, smooth
Lugubre (Fr., It.)   sad, mournful
Lustig (Ger.)   merrily, cheerfully

Maestoso (It.)   majestic, stately
Marcato (It.)   marked, accented

Marziale (It.)   martial, in the style of a march
Mässig (Ger.)   moderate (see *Tempo*)
Melancholique (Fr.)   melancholy
Meno (It.)   less
Mesto (It.)   sad, mournful
Misura (It.)   measure
    Senza misura   without measure, freely
Mit (Ger.)   with
Moderato (It.), *Modéré* (Fr.)   see *Tempo*
Molto (It.)   much, a great amount
Morendo (It.)   dying away
Mosso, Moto (It.), *Mouvement* (Fr.)   motion, movement
    Avec mouvement (Fr.)   with motion
    Con moto (It.)   with motion, rather quick

Non (It.)   not
Nostalgico (It.)   nostalgic

Ostinato (It.)   obstinate, continuing

Passionato (It.)   passionate
Passione (It.)   passion, feeling
Perdendosi (It.)   dying away
Pesante (It.)   heavy, ponderous
Piacevole (It.)   pleasing, agreeable
Più (It.)   more
Placido (It.)   placid, calm
Poco (It.)   a little
    Poco a poco   gradually
Polacca (It.)   a Polish dance
Pomposo (It.)   pompous, grand
Prestissimo (It.)   see *Tempo*
Presto (It.)   see *Tempo*

Rallentando (Rall.) (It.)   becoming gradually slower
Rasch (Ger.)   very fast, swift, spirited
Religioso (It.)   religiously, solemn
Retenu (Fr.)   held back
Risoluto (It.)   resolved, resolute, bold
Ritard (Rit.) (It.)   becoming gradually slower
Ritmico (It.)   rhythmically
Rubato (It.)   freely with respect to tempo
Ruhig (Ger.)   quiet, calm
Rustico (It.)   rural, rustic, coarse

Scherzando (It.)   playful, lively
Schleppend (Ger.)   dragging
Schmerzvollisch (Ger.)   painfully, dolorous
Schnell (Ger.)   fast
    Nicht zu schnell (Ger.)   not too fast
    So schnell wie möglich   as fast as possible
Schwerigkeit (Ger.)   heaviness, seriousness, severity, difficulty
Schwungvoll (Ger.)   animated, spirited
Sehnsucht (Ger.)   desire, ardor, longing, fervor
Sehr (Ger.)   very
Semplice (It.)   simple
Sempre (It.)   always, continuously
Sentimentale (It.)   sentimentally
Sentimento (It.)   sentimental

Sentito (It.)   expressive
Senza (It.)   without
Serioso (It.)   serious
Siciliano (It.)   graceful movement of a pastoral character
Simile (It.)   similarly, continue in the same manner
Slancio (It.)   vehemence
    Con slancio (It.)   impetuously
Solenne (It.)   solemn
Sordamente (It.)   muted, softly
Sospirando (It.)   sighing, doleful
Sostenuto (It.)   sustained, legato
Sotto voce (It.)   softly, in a subdued manner
Spasshaft (Ger.)   jokingly, playfully
Spirito (It.)   spirit, energy
Spiritoso (It.)   with spirit, energetic
Spirituoso (It.)   with religious feeling
Squillante (It.)   ringing
Stark (Ger.)   strong, vigorous, loud
    So stark wie möglich   as strong as possible

Tempo (It.)   time, relative speed or rate of the pulse or beat
    A tempo (It.)   once again in time

Chart of Relative Tempos
M.M.

40	Grave
	Largo
	Larghetto
	Lento
60	Adagio
	Adagietto
72	Andante
	Andantino
90	Moderato
	Allegretto
120	Allegro
140	Presto
208	Prestissimo

Tenuto (It.)   sustained, held out
Trascinando (It.)   dragging
Trés (Fr.)   very
Troppo (It.)   much
    Non troppo   not too much

Valse (Fr.)   waltz
Vienne (Fr.)   Vienna
    À la vienne   in the style of a Viennese waltz
Vif (Fr.)   lively
Vite (Fr.)   fast, quickly
Vivace (It.)   lively
Volkston, Im Volkston (Ger.)   in the manner of a folksong

Walzer (Ger.)   waltz
Wuth (Ger.)   madness, rage

Zart (Ger.)   gently, sweetly, tender, soft
Zeitmass (Ger.)   tempo
    Im Zeitmass   in tempo
Zierlich (Ger.)   neat, graceful
Zurückhaltend (Ger.)   ritard